I so did not want to edit this book, but I have to because there v
And yes editing this book is hard, a chore for some strange reaso
easiest book to edit, but this one is proving difficult to me for so... ....
listening to music can ease my mind and thoughts.

Maybe it's because I have no vibe, no yearning or desire to do anything with this book, hence I am finding it hard to edit. Plus my spirit isn't gnawing at me to edit it like it did book one.

I guess this is me.

Man is this book truly racist. And I truly don't like it; the beginning and the racism in the beginning. I truly can't get into it despite the truth that's in it. So be truly warned and read at your own risk.

And if time permits, I will try to add some stuff that is of no relevance to this book. Not to throw you off, but to kill the depressing mood this book brings.

And yes I am critical of my own work because I truly need all my books to be error free but I am bound by the laws of God – Good God. I cannot bring anyone into the mix.

Hey maybe in 2015 I can truly be free to write romance novels again but I highly doubt it. I am on one path and I think it's going to stay this way for a while.

Yes eventually the spiritual writing must stop but when is another issue and or story. But for now truly try to enjoy these books and let the musical references that are given truly soothe and comfort you daily.

Michelle Jean
December 06, 2014

I am the sun and the moon
I am comfort
Joy
Your paradise

I am the reigns you hold on to
The beam of light that lights your way

I am your hope
Truth
Rivers of water
Good and wholesome food

I am organic
Never plastic

I am big boned
Your Chubby Lumpkin

I am your queen
Your lover
Friend
Everything

I am your raisin in the sun
Well tanned; brown

I am natural
A natural beauty

I am temperamental
Got flare
Angry when pushed to the edge
A cussa
Hot headed

I am me
Free
Free to be me each and every day.

Michelle Jean
December 06, 2014

Man do I feel awful
Body losing strength
The first stages of the flu

Nose burning
Eyes I truly cannot say
Feel icky, yucky
Blaugh

Hate flu season
Truly hate to be sick
Now I am getting to hate life
Well the sickness of life anyway.

Day is dull and boring
Puppy driving me crazy
Need to give her away because I truly don't like her

She's annoying
Nasty
Messy
No wonder my daughter likes her
Say she's her puppy

She makes a mess everywhere
Dear God the poor destroyed toys
Stuffing everywhere

The weather is getting cold again but yet I can't run away.

Ah well maybe one day when I get fed up and return home.
Home to where because I am banned from going to Jamaica by Good God and Allelujah. So like many, I too am left in the cold. Oh well this is life I guess.

Blaugh, blaugh, blaugh.

Nothing funny about this because I was told Japan and Jamaica is going to be destroyed. When is the other story? Oh well this is the payment for their sins I guess - too much evil island wide. I guess they never thought of the sins of the past. They were not paid, hence the continual sins of the people on the island was added to the past sins of Jamaica. In all they did for sin, they never thought about payment of their forefathers and mothers sins. Never thought their sins would be added to those sins and then some. All the killing – bloodletting and the government truly has done nothing about it. PNP diss and JLP diss, the pedophilic activity, brutal rapes and killing have and has cost them their lives and place with Good God. Yes it's crying time for Jamaica hence truly woe be

unto them real soon. This time there is no one to save them. No one to say peace be unto you to stop death.

*I too can't return home and this is a pity. We did not listen to the cries of Marcus Mosiah Garvey and Bob Marley. We made Jamaica dirty hence the land is condemned; was deemed unclean – dirty by Good God and Allelujah himself. **So because of this, I truly don't want to be disobedient nor do I want to go to hell and burn. I have to stay out of this land until he Good God deems the island clean again.***

All that want to go home cannot. We are locked out indefinitely. Well not indefinitely because Jamaica can save self if they become 99.9% clean. But like I said, I have no faith and trust in my own; my own people. Too much obeah this and obeah that hence the voodoo nonsense will neva done. Too much eat a food business. Too much scamming and too much whaa whaa like dem a fiya truck; engine.

I cannot believe; no, I won't go there because millions of them prefer evil and fight for wicked and evil people instead of sustaining self and doing all that is good for self. Hence Demarco told you the way some of the people are in his song LOYAL featuring Busy Signal. Some of us are so bad mine and grudge full that you can't have anything lest you are set up and killed for it. Listen to FULFILLMENT TIME by Tony Tuff and Smokie Benz and listen to what they are talking about. Listen to Smokie Benz tell you what they are doing to babies. These things are reality. They do happen and it happens in Jamaica. Hence Jamaica has been deemed unclean; dirty by Good God himself. Hence the downfall of Jamaicans is due to Jamaicans and no one else but them. Many are wicked and evil hence they must go down in flames; the fires of hell literally. Now go to the internet and listen to Bob Marley's song Rastaman Chant and here how Babylon is being chanted down and it's a matter of time before Babylon falls because Babylon must fall down infinitely and indefinitely forever ever without end indefinitely. Their wickedness has and have gone on for far too long. So if Good God's children don't wake up and come back to ZION then truly woe be unto them because they too will go down in flames literally.

Zion will come down to earth to shield and protect her own and if the people of Zion don't listen then it's their waterloo and they will miss their calling literally.

ONWARDS I GO BECAUSE I'VE STRAYED ALREADY.

They care not for their souls hence millions have none; they've become walking duppies. Sad yes, but this is reality I guess. When we put others over self and God this is what you get; a lawless society that craves death and do all for death.

A man say hate your brother because he's not politically correct; he's on the wrong side, you hate the man for this. Some even kill for their political affiliation. But with all this said; no one truly cares. No one added up the cost and costs of their sins island wide.

Dem a PNP diss and JLP dat. They follow their political leaders to their deaths without knowing they too are going to die and become extinct because of the wrongs they've done; do.

In all they do, (people of Jamaica) they've aligned themselves with sin and now sin will take them down real soon.

As a human being you cannot say you represent your people and or the people and have a political divide. You are wrong because the motto of Jamaica say, "OUT OF MANY ONE PEOPLE." So if we are one people then why aren't all treated as one; fairly?

Why are we divided politically and socioeconomically?

Why is there different rules for the different classes?

Why does one party favour his people over the next party?

Should both parties not work for the better good of the people and country and not destroy them and the country?

So how can we be one when the laws do not favour all?

I don't know. Maybe it's my sickness getting to my head but who knows because I truly do not feel like myself.

My world is different, odd. To you it's crazy. Hey some of you are saying I am a demon. Some of you are saying I am the anti-Christ, but I truly don't care nor do I give a damn. I am anti religion hence I am anti death. I am for life – all good and true life, hence I live for good and true life; honest and clean life not death. I care not for negative energy and death knows this. So because death knows this, I do my best not to walk on the road of death; evil. I already live in the valley and the shadow of death here on earth and it is this; death's valley and his shadow that I do my best to escape. Good God and Allelujah told me to write a book, he did not tell me to give humanity and or his people religion because we both know that religion; all religion is death of the body and spirit; soul. So because of this, I refuse to give humanity and or his Good God's people death – religion. No one can make me give you something to kill you. No one should live for death, you should live for life. Know this, with Good God and Allelujah, human life does not boil down to the dollar bill and it should not be this way with man; humanity. All life is worth it no matter the way you feel. Yes we feel pain but our hardships and pain is not due to God – Good God, it is due to man and his greed; evils.

God – Good God did not make stress we as humans did.

We live for greed because we are not content and happy with what we have. We have to have what the next man or woman has. Well bleep that. I truly don't want what the next man or woman has. I need my own and I am going to work for my own. The mate I need I tell Good God the qualities I am looking for; hence I will wait on him to find me that right person. And yes I told him I truly do not want or need any Babylonian. Not because of hate but truly out of respect for him and yes to an extent my ancestors of old. We did not listen hence many got cast out with Adam and Eve and I refuse to make the same mistake as them, hence I listen. And will continue to listen until I return home to him in truth and good faith; honesty.

Listen there are no dead people in Good God's kingdom and abode. God – Good God is not dead so why the hell should I live my life like the dead? Come on now.

To you I am the insane one but I truly do not care nor do I give a damn. All I know is that I do not want to be in places that we call civilized societies because we are not civilized, we are uncivilized hence we destroy; kill. We are murderers hence we invade other lands and destroy; kill in the interest of you. We spy on others and say we are protecting self. How the hell can you protect self if you are spying on the next land? Are you not in sighting strife with you and that and or the next land? Are you not setting yourself up for war; mistrust when it comes to that land? So how can we say we are civilized when we have trust issues? We tell lies on the next land or man to make ourselves look good and this is wrong. Hence when truth comes, the truth is not accepted by the many and or the one percent that claim rulership of this earth; world. Anyone that speaks the truth must be eliminated at all cost in this day and time and this is sad. Hence the devil and his people do not want the truth to be known. When you start educating people and telling them the truth they do all to eliminate you because you are disturbing their nest. See evil does not think of the consequences of their actions because to them there is no God. They are supreme because they created societies of men for them and them alone. They control and dominate you hence you are told what to wear, what to eat, who to date, which educational institution you must go to, what church you must go to amongst other things. Satan and Hell does not exist in many of their books. Satan and hell is something that is made up to scare man; the have nots. But little do they know that there is a hell and their life in hell will be a harsh and brutal; long.

People it matters not if my God is not your god. You are going the face the wrath of hell real soon and there isn't a damned thing billions of you can do about it. You created hell with your sins.

You created the time you are going to spend in hell because you sinned. You did not pay for your sins by asking forgiveness of the one (s) you erred.

Your hell is your own and not mine. So when these billionaires and millionaires are dancing and playing a joyful noise with sin, sin is smiling because sin knows in time they are all going to die and pay the piper. No one that is evil can escape the grave; death. And truly don't go there with cremation of the flesh and bones. Cremation cannot kill the spirit. No one in the living have this authority. The only one that can kill the spirit is death. This is his job, hence I tell you I worry not about wicked and evil people because I know hell is there for them and they will have hell to pay.

No one is stronger than death when it comes to death. No, this is not true because death can be stopped. The valley of death belongs to death because we as humans created death's valley with our sins. The more we sin it's the hotter the flames and or fires of hell gets. Good God has nothing to do with death hence death cannot go into the abode of Good God nor can death take Good God's children to hell with him. Hence Death is not all powerful Good God is. In the abode of death, death is all powerful because this is his and her domain and Good God does not interfere with them. Has nothing to do with them. And no you cannot travel back and forth from one realm to the next. Good is separated from evil hence evil cannot find the realm and or abode of God in the spiritual world even though they are side by side. Good God can and does keep death at bay when it comes to his children, so in truth Death is not more powerful than God – Good God and Allelujah because his children; those who are ordained by Him Good God can stop death in his and her tracks in the physical and spiritual. And I hope I've explained this correctly so not to confuse you.

Hence I ask you, are we not barbarians that live in barbaric societies?

We are not an obedient society but a lawless one. And because of this, I truly do not want to be amongst anyone. I need to be amongst my truly peaceful and truly good, honest and clean own.

I cannot take the anger and hate anymore. Everyone fighting based on religion, colour and race – hue; the hue of man hence hue man (human).

We fight and hate based on sexual affiliation. But with all this said, humanity has and have forgotten about the cross that they have to bare. Hence we are the ones to die on crosses; the cross of death not Jesus. Therefore the true Jews could not accept Jesus; death. A true Jew know death hence they walk away from death and all that is wicked and evil. This cross of death billions of you accept globally and this is sad. This is your death; your cross that will see you go to hell for millions, hundreds of millions of years including billions and trillions before your eventual death; extinction. Trust me, I do not want to be society today nor do I want or need to be any of you. As humans many of you have and has sinned reckless and rude and now the time comes for you to pay.

Know that your sins are your crosses; the different ways you will be tormented in hell before your spirit dies. And yes this is why your book of sin told you Jesus died on a cross. He did not die to save you like your book of sin (Holy Bible) tells you. He lied about him being the Son of God and he lied about him being the son of man because when it is all said and done, no one can die to save you from death if you of yourself have sinned. Your sins are recorded on your sin record and if you are not a part of Good God's world and kingdom you cannot be saved; meaning he cannot save you because you do not belong to him Good God. If you believe in death and worship death then you belong to death not life. So know you because if you do not do all in goodness and in truth to make amends for your sins; truly good luck when your spirit leaves your body because you are doomed literally in the spiritual world. Trust me when I tell you many are balling like a bitch in the grave right now because of the Jesus and Allah bullshit. You cannot say you love god and or of peace and kill. You are not of God you are of death and you are going to die. There are no ands ifs or buts about this. This is your true reality. And in truth Jesus never existed in the way you think. Death exist hence you have BLACK AND WHITE DEATH LITERALLY. Your physical and spiritual Jesus. Yes the two deaths. Female death is different hence billions of you know nothing about her.

Like I've said time and time again, life is given, we are the ones to give it away to death and this is sad. No one wants to die but yet we refuse to stop sinning, stop lying to self and others.

Yes the lies have to stop and it begins with us. Death has his job to do and you cannot stop death when he comes; she comes. So truly good luck to you

Yes it's Saturday and I am so trying to fight the flu. I do not want it to be full blown because I know the toll it will take on my body.

Oh God, I truly do not need to be around people right now. For some strange reason, I need to be by myself communicating with you my way. Man do I need some devotional time with you; just you and me in nature relishing the peace and quiet around us.

It's as if I have no feeling when it comes to wicked and evil people. Hence I am listening to WORLD GONE MAD by Richie Stephens featuring Gentleman and Alborosie. I need to listen to this song again because what they are singing about is right. The people of the world has and have gone crazy because many are plagued by suicidal tendencies, many are plagued with depression – stress overload.

Many are abused and killed especially kids.

Our food is chemically induced and chemically prepared. Who wouldn't go mad; crazy over time with all the chemicals we ingest, chemicals that alter our genes and change our physical DNA.

Youths; children less than ten years old stealing and smoking Mary Jane. Dear God I truly need to get out of here because you cannot control the youths. They have no soul. As citizens of the world, how can we say the children are the future when at a young age they (our children) are strung out on drugs and stealing? You don't even know who is strapped from who is not strapped. Hence I must quickly flee. Do not want to be caught up in the struggle – troubles and the global economic crisis that's heading our way. And Good God you truly know what I mean underneath the parable. I truly need rescuing because when it comes to money the heart of man is cold – wicked and evil for real.

Dear God we listened to evil and look at the cost. Satan and his people won over man. We bought into his lies and like Eve (Evening) we became locked out of your house Good God indefinitely.

His book of sin – man's so called holy bible did the damage. Now humanity must pay and pay with their lives just like Eve (Evening) literally.

We've over populated the earth and look at the cost. People needing jobs to feed their families and can't find any. Some are burdens to the system. But shortly the systemic burdens of man will come to an end and man – billions of men and women including children must fend for self – their own.

All I have to say is, truly good luck if you're in countries that are cold.

Look how we've cut down the trees, trees you put there to help us and save us. But as humans we care not for anything. We care not for the world we live in. If we did, the world would not be in such a mess and the people of the world wouldn't be so insane.

War, War, no more rumors of war but war.
Economic divide
Social unrest
Soon to be economic collapse globally.

Yes this is the final days and it's not pretty for man. Many lives will be lost because of the choices we made here on earth.

How can we save self Good God when everything has gone wrong?
How can we save self when we don't even know you?
Can't obey you.

Yes it's a shame because we listened to the wrong one hence giving up our soul; everything.

Truly look upon us Good God because we more than need you. We need care.

We need your advice and direction. Hell is not pretty but yet we willingly kill and or sin to get there without knowing the cost and or penalty of our wrongs - sins.

AND TO THE WORLD, PEOPLE OF THE WORLD, BLACK PEOPLE ARE

NOT SLAVES. WE DID NOT COME HERE AS SLAVES BECAUSE GOD – GOOD GOD MADE NO SLAVES. HUMANS LIED TO US AND CONQUERED US THEN MADE US THEIR SLAVES. MANY OF US SOLD THEIR BIRTHRIGHT TO YOU BECAUSE OF YOUR LIES AND EVIL PROMISES. (JACOB AND ESAU). YES OUR ANCESTORS MADE THE WRONG CHOICE IN TRUSTING YOU, BUT BLACKS ARE TRULY AND INDEFINITELY NOT SLAVES. YOU OFFERED A PRICE AND OUR ANCESTORS WENT AGAINST GOD – GOOD GOD AND WHEN WE DID THIS, WE TRIGGERED OUR OWN DOWNFALL; DESTRUCTION. HENCE OUR HELL AND SUFFERINGS ON EARTH BY YOU THE WHITE AND INDIAN AND OR BABYLONIAN DEVILS OF OLD AND TODAY.

WE WERE THE DISOBEDIENT ONES THAT DID NOT LISTEN; REFUSE TO LISTEN TO THE WISDOM AND KNOWLEDGE OF GOOD GOD AND ALLELUJAH. YOUR GOD AND PEOPLE HATED US HENCE YOU THE WHITE DEVIL'S PUT ENMITY BETWEEN US. YOU CALL US AND CLASS US WITH ALL NEGATIVE STEREOTYPES WHEN YOU OF YOURSELF KNOW THAT YOU'RE THE EVIL ONES THAT CAN'T LIVE GOOD WITH ANYONE.

YOU THE WHITE RACE; TRUE WHITE RACE (Babylonians, Egyptians, Arabs, Americans, Ethiopians, Iraqis, Iranians, Somalia's, Saudis, Nodites, Lebanese, Pakis to name a few) WANT WHAT WE HAVE AND IF YOU CAN'T GET IT, YOU KILL TO GET IT; DESTROY. YOU DESIGN AND CREATE DISEASE INFESTED FOOD – YOUR HANDOUT THAT YOU SAY IS GOOD AND GIVE IT TO HUMANITY TO KILL THEM. YOUR OIL IS NOT CLEAN EITHER BECAUSE IT DOES CAUSE CANCER. AND IN FACT NOTHING THAT YOU DO IS GOOD BECAUSE THIS IS HOW YOU CATCH US AND KILL US. YOU CONTAMINATE THE FOOD AND MEDICINES YOU GIVE TO US WITH YOUR DISEASES THEN TURN AROUND AND SAY THESE DISEASES COME FROM AFRICA – BLACK PEOPLE; THE BLACK RACE AND WE THE BLACK RACE ARE TOO FOOLISH TO SEE THIS. YES THERE ARE MORE DISEASES TO COME. DISEASES THAT WILL PLAGUE BLACK LANDS BECAUSE I DREAMNT IT. HENCE TRULY WOE BE UNTO MAN BECAUSE OF YOUR WICKEDNESS AND DECEIT; LIES THAT MORE THAN DECEIVE BUT KILL.

YOU TAINT OUR SKIN COLOUR BUT LIKE I SAID, TRULY WOE BE UNTO MAN BECAUSE BLACK IS MORE THAN BEAUTIFUL. IT'S

UNIVERSAL, HENCE THE DARKNESS IN THE HEAVENS – SKY AND UNIVERSE INCLUDING EARTH.

YOU CANNOT COMPREHEND OUR HOLINESS HENCE YOU DEFILE US AND GET US TO DEFILE OUR BEAUTIFUL AND GORGEOUS SKIN. BUT NO MORE BECAUSE THE HARVEST COMES AND LIKE I SAID, BILLIONS OF YOU ARE SLATED FOR HELL. HENCE HELL, YOUR MARK OF THE BEAST (666) IS TIME AND THAT TIME HAS EXPIRED. NOW DEATH WILL TRULY TALK AND WALK – SMILE WHILST TAKING THE LOTS OF YOU TO HELL WITH HIM. SO NO MATTER HOW YOU TRY TO CHANGE THE RECORDS TO SAY YOU THE WHITE RACE, GOOD GOD WILL MAKE THE TRUTH BE KNOWN. THE TRUTH CANNOT CHANGE HENCE TRUTH IS EVERLASTING LIFE. NO MATTER THE TIME THE TRUTH WILL FOREVER EVER REMAIN THE SAME INFINITELY AND INDEFINITELY WITHOUT END. SO NO MATTER HOW YOU TARGET US GOOD GOD AND ALLELUJAH WILL FOREVER SAVE US; HIS OWN, HIS OWN PEOPLE. HE WILL LET THE TRUTH BE KNOWN NO MATTER HOW LONG IT TAKES.

SO TRULY STOP SAYING WE THE BLACK RACE ARE SLAVES BECAUSE YOU THE WHITE RACE AND INDIAN RACE (BABYLONIAN RACE) COLONIZED EVERY BLACK LAND AND GAVE US YOUR NASTY RELIGIONS OF SINS TO FURTHER DEFILE US AND BRING US TO HELL. NO AFRICAN LAND IS SLAVE LAND, THEY ARE BLACK LAND. BLACK LANDS SOME OF YOU CONQUERED AND STOLE FROM BLACK PEOPLE. SO PLEASE STOP YOUR LIES AGAINST US THE BLACK RACE AND PEOPLE. EVERY LAND ON EARTH BELONGS TO BLACK PEOPLE; US, SO TRULY DO NOT TRY. NONE (NO LAND) BELONG TO WHITE PEOPLE. ALL YOU'VE MANAGED TO DO IS EXERCISE YOUR WAR MENTALITY BY ROBBING AND KILLING BLACK PEOPLE AND TAKING THEIR OWN; LANDS – EARTH. AND I AM FED UP NOW MAN. FED UP OF THE LOTS OF YOU AND YOUR LIES AND DECEIT.

STOP CALLING US SLAVES BECAUSE WE CREATED IT ALL. FIND YOUR OWN DAMNED PLANET AND HOME IF YOU CAN. WAIT THERE'S HELL FOR EACH AND EVERY ONE OF YOU. YOUR NASTY BIBLE – BOOK JUST TELL YOU HOW TO KILL GOD'S CHILDREN AND TAKE WHAT BELONGS TO THEM. SO TRULY DON'T TRY YOUR SHIT WITH ME. AND FOR ALL OF YOU WHITES THAT ARE SAYING I AM BLEEPING RACIST TRULY KISS MY ASS.

AND FOR YOU BLACKS THAT ARE JUMPING FOR JOY AND SAY SEE WE THE BLACK RACE OWN IT ALL CAN KISS MY ASS AS WELL BECAUSE SOME WHITES ARE BLACK AND MANY OF YOU BLACKS ARE WHITE. AND YOU CAN THANK ETHIOPIA FOR ORIGINALLY SELLING OUT THE BLACK RACE HENCE BLACKS CAN BE FOUND IN NOD – INDIA UNTIL THIS DAY. KNOW THE TRUTH AS WELL AS YOUR DAMNED HISTORY. NOW YOU KNOW SO DO BETTER AS SO CALLED CIVILIZED BEINGS. SORRY YOU ARE ONLY HUMANS AND NOT BEINGS BECAUSE THE FLESH IS ALL YOU KNOW. HENCE YOUR FLESH IS THE BEGINNING OF YOUR LIFE AND NOT THE SPIRIT AND OR BOTH FOR THOSE OF YOU WHO TRULY KNOW.

Michelle Jean
October 04 and 18, 2014
December 6 and 7, 2014

Good God what is true praise of you?

What is the true truth of you and why do I see this Black Woman in this spiritual church?

What does she have to do with me?

Yes her congregation is black; filled with black people of both genders (male and female) but what does she want with me?

Who is she to me and why does she use a church – spiritual church? You know me and churches but with all this said Good God, why can't she truly leave me alone?

I know not of her but yet she is around me. Who is she Good God?

Do I need to know her?

Do I need to know her church?

Do I need to know what the spiritual church represent?

Good God, I cannot comprehend the scope of her and I truly don't think I know how to. I want to flee from her but yet I am confused and drawn to her at times. The world is there for me and if I leave the avenue I am on, the world will be lost to me. So I have to stay focused in my life but it's hard to do. Things are coming left and right at me hence my dreams are becoming more confusing. Losing you is not an option I know this by why her? What does she want with me?

I have to come to you because I am listening William Murphy's song PRAISE IS WHAT I DO. The song isn't doing much for me but it's a nice song. I guess in a way I am sad because you have these men and women with beautiful voice that's lifting their voice to Jesus and not to you; her.

We know Jesus did not exist but yet we believe in him Jesus. All your children from what I saw are females not males. So if this is the case, where did Jesus come from? Yes I know it's a Babylonian thing – mother and child that's worldwide. It's a shame and pity hence we can't truly know you. Know how beautiful and good you are.

We sing praises to other gods. Praise that are so beautiful and forget about you; but yet we expect you to save us. We praise other gods and give them thanks and truly neglect you and this is sad. You're the one to provide for us, but yet we can't thank you properly; do right and well; true by you.

As for her, I know she has a clean church in the spiritual realm but I cannot bring myself to associate myself with this church. Not because of cleanliness but because of truth. The physical churches of the world tell lies and deceive their members and I refuse to associate myself with deceit. I am leery of spiritual churches Good God hence I have to stay the way I am for the betterment of me and you in the physical and spiritual world. Until I know more about her I will speak of her in depth. But for now I can't. I just have to wonder about her and what she want and need with me.

Dear Lord I truly thank you for this morning because in my hour of sickness you showed me many things. But it is beyond me why we as black people cannot listen and change our dirty linen of self.

We sing praises to other gods and leave you out. When I hear some of these gospel music; songs it does hurt me that we've excluded you in all that we do. We give other gods the praise and I am so disheartened by it.

Tell me Good God, why can't we give you the true praise?

Why can't we lift our voices to you?

Yes I truly want to cry to see how we've neglected you in songs; all that we do.

It grieves me to know that you gave some of us these beautiful voices and we use it to praise other gods, other gods that mean us no good. These gods are not ours, but yet we praise them anyway.

No Good God, I can't imagine how you feel to hear these beautiful voices lifting up praise to other gods.

It hurts me; grieves me like I've said and it's not good.

I so need you to get these praise because praising and glorifying you is so wonderful and true. Good God why can't it be? Why can't I sing you praise of joy more beautiful than these people?

Yes I have words and I guess these words are my beautiful praise and voice unto you despite the numerous mistakes in these books. Mistakes I miss and this is sad. Ah Good God you are my way and I truly love you. Nothing is going to change this even though I gave you a mandate of 2015 January 1 (first) to step aside and leave you and death to do what you need to do in regards to humanity globally (our good and evil).

I can't go on any further with this because life is worth living and I truly need to live life good and clean. Yes I need to build you your mega mansion but I truly do not have the funds to build this mansion for you and you are doing nothing to help me financially. Hence I have to put your home on hold. Maybe the one you ordain to save humanity will build you your true home.

I am truly sorry if I've failed you but your mansion with me will always be my good and true heart and my more than unconditional love of truth for you and of you. No one can sever and or damage this mansion hence you are my good all and good everything; true lifeline and life jacket. Yu cut to fit hence you more than truly suit me – fit me.

Like I said, the dream world is getting weirder for me. Just this morning, December 07, I dreamt about Ebola. Had two dreams in one night about it. Oh man because I can't tell you the full dream because segments are missing.

Dreamt the world map and Canada is going to get hit with the virus. On the map Australia and the South Pacific was shown but I am not sure if the virus hit there. I think these lands had the cure but I am so not one hundred percent sure. The virus became airborne in Canada and it affected babies. This white guy who reminded me of Josh Stamberg had the cure. He had two containers. The containers looked like those Air Wick thingimigingees that has the gel in it. With the virus becoming airborne I was sprayed with the virus and so were the people around me including these two babies. The virus did not affect me or him but it affected the babies and that's when I figured out the containers; two of them he had were the cure for the virus. He gave the babies the cure and was reminding about out East – Eastern Canada where they came from.

There is more to the dream people but I cannot remember all. I know there were airports but I cannot fully remember how these airports played a part in this virus. But at the end he gave the people of the land the cure to plant in the soil so that the virus would not affect the food and they were happy because they did plant and the land did yield good food.

So people and family I truly do not know because like I said there are more diseases to be unleashed on man – humanity and this is truly sad; a tragedy that man have and has become so vile and wicked that human life is valued not. Thus the killing fields has truly begun but this killing field is not done with bombs and ammunitions but with genetic warfare – man made diseases. Hence the wickedness of the devil and his people is not done.

Michelle Jean
October 8, 2014 and December 07, 2014

In all I truly have to thank you for all Good God.

You are Allelujah – All. And I truly thank you for my life and keeping me thus far in the physical and spiritual. It's been a long and rough road – hard but I am here with you.

You know you've been trying to tell me how black people don't listen all night and you know you are right. We truly don't listen. But despite our non listening ways, you are still with us and I am truly glad for that. Though I don't understand nor comprehend why you're still around people that truly don't listen.

Why God?

Why do you stay with self absorbed and stiff necked people that think the world owes them something because of slavery?

Like I've said, we were the ones to let the devil in and we are still letting the devil in. Eve listened to him and look at the cost to her and her children; people until this day.

We are still doing the same bullshit today with the Jesus bullshit; lies and nonsense. A dead man cannot save you. He's bleeping dead. Once the spirit hits the grave and if you do not have more good than evil on your record and or slate, then you can only go down to hell and burn. You cannot go up to see Good God and Allelujah. Come on now. You sinned and you are accountable and or responsible for your sins. If you do not cover your sins in the living – here on earth, you cannot cover them and or make amends for them in the grave. Come on now. Know the truth because this is your life. So truly take care of it. No one can petition Good God and Allelujah for the next man's and or persons sins if they are not ordained to do so. Meaning if Good God and Allelujah did not ordain and or trust you to save his children you cannot. The person he Good God and Allelujah ordains have to live clean. They must be truthful and just to all life regardless of ills.

Like I've said, look at a dead body. It has no life so why would anyone want to become like this; dead? Oh well, I guess we have not heard that it pays to listen to the good words of Good God and Allelujah.

*You know and see the storm and Good God have been protecting us for this storm for thousands of years, billions for some. But like disobedient children, we continue on our sinful and evil pathway believing someone is going to save us at the last hour. Read again, **Good God have been protecting us from the storm for thousands of years.** He Good God can no longer do this (protect us). We did not choose him, hence we continue to sin whilst believing someone is going to come swooping down from the sky and save us. The only thing that is going to swoop down from the sky is Wormwood as talked about in Revelations of your book of sin. When wormwood hits earth what then? So truly think because Earth is on a collision course with death and when all hits at once no one will be left. Not even your 144 million. There is a gateway to time that I dreamt about and a man – white man came through the portal. I cannot tell you much about him, but this break in the space time continuum is not for wicked and evil people in my view but I could be wrong but I truly don't think so now. Good, good people have a pathway that they must prepare for because like I've told you, man was to walk to Good God* *and Allelujah in the flesh and spirit. Yes as in our human form; but we cannot do this dirty, we have to do this clean.* **_Hence you were told to live in spirit and in truth._** *You may not comprehend this nor do I fully, but once I do I will let you know. This key and or pathway is what the devil wants but he cannot have it nor will it (this key) be given to him and his people. Hence the harvest comes to destroy all wicked and evil life and spirit. You need to know this hence it's imperative for you to know about spiritual life. Yes the upward and downward triangle.* <u>*If you are good never point your triangle down, but point it up because life – good and true life go up not down. Do not point a cross because like I've told you, there are no crosses in her spiritual church. The cross is what your God – Jesus the one you believe in died on so truly don't wear it. When you wear the cross you are acknowledging death hence death can truly take you. True evil invert the cross but either way the cross is death. There is a Southern Cross which is totally different from the cross of the church; hence I am hoping to get to this cross in depth once the information is fully given to me.*</u>

Is the key to life and death an actual key?

I saw it as an actual key. So yes, the key to life and death is an actual key. Like I've said, we are the disobedient ones that refuse to listen. Hence we are like unto the children of Noah. All died expect for Noah and his family. This according to your book of sin and whoredom.

Good God, just know that you are my angel, good food and all. You've seen me through many storms and I truly thank you. I know it's not easy to listen to you. I am a testament of this. Trust me, well you know that many times I want to disobey you but I am trying to hold on and not hurt you.

<u>*Last night I was reminded of Bob Marley when he said in one of his songs, "no matter how they kill us, we will keep resurfacing." And you also confirmed to me that no matter what they do to the black race you will always be with us.*</u>

Yes I know we are your people but to be honest with you Good God, the heartache and pain of seeing what others are doing to the black race is disheartening to me. Why Good God?

Why?

Why do they hate us so much?

Is it jealousy?
Or is it fear?

Fear of the unknown and uncertainty? Good God I know you, you are certain, so why have the black race become the target of such hatred and pain?

Why did we give up certainty and sure for evil, sin and death; the death of self?

Why put us through all of this? Our ancestors went through it and now we are going through it again. It seems like it's hunting season globally and the black race globally is the target. We've become preys for the many and this is wrong.

You know it's funny how we say we love you God, but yet in all of our loving; we hate and treat others unfair. I know some of these books are harsh – it's the harsh reality of humanity but yet, I truly don't know if they will understand; comprehend. Good God tell me what right does the good and pure at heart have to save anyone that is wicked and evil?

Look at the human race globally Good God and tell me what right do we have to hate and kill each other?

You did not put enmity against the races; man did that all on their own. So why do we blame you for our wrongs?

Why tell lies on you like this Good God? Enmity was already there come on now. North hated South and they still do and this is not right. What wrong did we do to the North for them to hate us so? They have their gods and we are not interfering with them, so why are they imposing their dirty values on us and interfering with us? Why are they taking you from us? Come on now.

The viruses have been unleashed now. The scorpion kings will kill and they are killing without mercy because man did design and create them in their laboratories. Soon they (humanity) will not be able to contain them. Hence the second woe of man – humanity globally is sounded. I give the order for the trumpet of death to blow because it is weeping season yet again. Allelujah, Good God man truly knows not what they have done.

Death walks now and death will claim the lives of man because man – humanity made it so. Sins and evils, yes the wickedness of man globally.

Evil knows what they were doing but yet with all they have done, evil and wicked people continue on with their evil and wicked ways. I guess they cannot see their own deaths. They don't know that they are going to die in the flesh and go to hell to truly face hell in the spirit. I guess some think hell is just like a holiday where you can vacation in the best hotels and eat the best of food even drive the most expensive car and lay with the most beautiful of women. Pity they don't know that Satan and or the devil lied to them. There hell will be brutal; hence their time spent in hell will be long and painful before their eventual extinction. They fear not hell because they don't believe in hell. Many say hell does not exist and this is wrong because you and I both know that there is a hell and it's not pretty. We are both physical and spiritual beings and once our life in the physical is done, our spirit must answer for the wrongs we have done on earth in the afterlife.

Hence I worry not about my enemies nor do I worry about your enemies Good God because we both know there is a hell and there is going to be hell to pay when death comes for them literally. Once this is over, woe be unto billions because true pain starts for them.

But with all that I know Good God, how can I trust humanity to do right and good by you?

How can I trust humanity to save self and live Good God when we sin so much?

There is a price to pay when it comes to our sins. Hence the wages (pay) of sin is death; indefinite and forever ever death. You do not hurt others and think you are going to get away with it. You won't, hence there's a hell; a true hell to pay.

Ooh Good God, I truly don't know. What I do know is that I truly do not want or need to live amongst wicked and evil people that truly don't know you. I want and need to escape the physical and spiritual madness of it all and alive in goodness and in truth with you forever ever indefinitely. But I cannot do this with the present state earth is in. I truly cannot stand to see the hurt and hate of man by wicked and evil people anymore. It's too painful hence I must find your true opening that leads me to you positively in flesh and spirit indefinitely. I so want to devote some time to you Good God, but how do I escape the madness of this world and find a place that is clean and true for us?

I need you to save black people Good God. I need you to truly save Africa because in all that we are going through in the West by the hands of the wicked many; you cannot let Africa fall apart anymore. We've been robbed enough. So truly save those who want saving; those who truly belong to you. Come on now. The West is collapsing so the target land is now Africa. Eradicate a few million blacks, revamp the land and take it. Own all the resources of Africa by setting up big business there and pay the people (whomever is left) next to nothing. This is the intention of the evil many in the west and east. Hence I am depending on you Good God and Allelujah to let all that these wicked and evil people do backfire on them indefinitely forever ever without end. So truly open the eyes of blacks, so that we can be free to govern and educate ourselves in goodness and in truth in a good and positive way forever ever without end indefinitely for more than infinite and indefinite lifetimes and generations universally in the physical and spiritual including earth.

Africa don't see the hatred towards them by the West and Western societies including some Eastern and or European lands; societies. Open their eyes Good God and let Africans globally reclaim their own in goodness and in truth. Do not let them be fooled anymore because I am tired of the hate and propaganda. You gave us Africa and Africa is engrained in our genes; DNA. Hence the enemy created walls to block the truth of our DNA. But in all that they do, they cannot block, change or alter the spirit – the true life and DNA of man – humanity. Hence they put enmity between their seed and thy seed Good

God. This according to their book of sin and lies — Genesis; their lying, whoring and incestual beginning.

Oh Good God my writing fails me because my hand is giving way. Tell me something Good God, why do I feel like you are against Africa?

Why do I see Tata's face in my head?

Is Africa not worthy of prayer and goodness anymore?

Is your blessings and truth being taken from them more and more?

Good God our spiritual DNA is our right and that right is you. Hence no matter how they kill us, they cannot kill our spirit — our true life and true DNA. We will resurface no matter how long it takes physically and spiritually.

Good God we've been raped enough.

We've been murdered and humiliated enough. And now the children of the land are going to feel it because of wicked and evil people and their man made diseases. Good God can't the evils of these wicked and evil scientists, physicists, governments; politicians, bankers and financiers turn back on them infinitely and indefinitely without end forever ever? We the black race; true black race did not design or create these diseases of wickedness. Nor did we create bombs and nuclear weapons to kill. Wicked and evil people including wicked and evil governments commissioned their people to design and create these deadly weapons to kill; wipe out nations. So Good God, can we not turn these people's wickedness and evils back on them? Come on now.

I know Africa did you wrong originally and this hurt you have not forgotten nor have you forgiven. This pain is hard to heal but you have to heal. You have to come clean and do for you and them. You have to find a way to truly forgive them for what they have done to you in the past and what they are doing to you today.

Listen the people of the world have sinned wicked and rude, but what gives them, humans the right to take a life; kill?

Isn't life sacred and precious to you, so why allow these people to go on a killing spree?

Let evil and wicked people suffer the fate of their own wickedness, evils and sins.

Good God why should they hurt others and tell lies on other people; races and they are the ones designing and creating evil things to destroy and kill people in society. Life is precious, so why let the enemy continue to take our life and need; you from us? You are precious to us, so why are you allowing wicked and evil people to push you further from us?

Good God I know it's not my place to say and plea but why us?

Why the black race?

Why do they have to treat us so unjust; worse than animals?

Why do they have to abuse and kill us?

<u>*We've done them nothing but yet they hurt us and give us their gods of sorrow and death to worship; praise. Then they have the gaul to say if we do not accept their dead and lying gods, we are going to go to hell and die. Good God these gods are not ours, so why should we bow down to them or even accept them?*</u>

Why should we give you up for hell?

<u>*When we walk away from you and accept these gods we are sinning against you. And this is truly not fair to us. Hence why should we give you up to become dead like them?*</u>

Why should we give you up to become truly abandoned wonderers (nomads) like them?

<u>*Why should we give you up to join them in hell and die in the like manner of them?*</u>

Why should we have to give you up to be deprived and destitute like them?

We have a home and that home is with you Good God so help us the best way you can.

The pain is there Good God and I know you have a bone to pick with Africa but despite this bone, you have to do right by your people. You cannot leave them alone.

Yes I know the hurt and pain but heal, truly heal this pain, your pain in a good and true way. The hurt must stop hence I am asking for true peace between you and Africa. I am asking for forgiveness for them because they truly did you wrong and have forgotten the wrong and wrongs they've done unto you. You gave them the truth of you and instead of taking care of this truth and cherishing it, they sold you out and allowed the devil to enslave them and reduce them to rubble until this day. Yes I know your anger but quell it for my sake and their sake. Let it be done Good God, truly let the anger within you be done. Michelle Jean

The enemies are there and they are causing us to sin and this is not fair to us nor is it fair to you. I truly do not want and need their gods because their gods are not ours; you are our God, our right and I refuse to have them take you from me. So why should I subject myself to sin and disrespect you? Tell me something, how is this right and fair; just when it comes to me and you? Why should I give up my life for them? They are not giving up their dead gods for you; so why should I give up Life – my true and good sweat heart of a God for them? They are not worth it, so why would I take my life from you? Oh God how can I beg for wicked and evil people knowing the atrocities they've done to other races – people? Yes I beg for Africa but in truth what right do I have to do so; beg for them knowing the wickedness of their past and their wickedness today?

Tell me Good God and the people of your world, how do you live with yourselves knowing the injustice of man unto man?

How do you smile or even hold your head up knowing and seeing the wickedness and evils of man globally and economically?

How can you live with yourself knowing that evil has and have taken billions from you? Yes I know billions do not belong to you but it's not fair to me and your people. We did not ask these people for their dead gods because you, the God of Life is my right; our true and good right.

You are not dead, so why should I accept death?

Why should I be fed the lies of death and be like the deceived?

You are the right of your true and good people and I refuse to accept death and his people over you. You cannot make me do this (accept them); hence I stake my claim of you right this minute in goodness and in truth. I am glued to you and you know this, so truly reclaim us; me you and our people in goodness and in truth. We are a true family and I refuse any disruption from evil when it comes to me and you and our true people.

There is an imbalance already and like I've said; let the children of death go. Good God you cannot protect and beg us anymore to listen to you.

You cannot violate yourself anymore when it comes to us and them. If your true children refuse to listen, let them the hell go. Let them go to hell and burn like you did Eve (Evening) long ago.

You are clean and you can no longer struggle with dirty people; people who do not want to save self and you.

You can no longer struggle and waste your precious time on people who want to continuously live on both sides of the fence and when it suits them they jump ship and come on your side at the last minute. This is not right to you nor is it right or just when it comes to your people; those who have been taking the blunt of the force by wicked and evil people including spirits. Good God you know the storm hence it's time now for us to find safety and rest from this brutal storm (harvest) that's coming. We are true love and we must protect self and help each other until the storm is over. Truly listen to the STORM IS OVER by R. Kelly because the storm is truly over. We cannot battle evil we must let all evil go. It's time; time for death to take his and her own to hell literally.

We cannot continue to let death destroy and kill. Life, good life is the answer to all, hence everyone that is evil must answer for the evils that they have done.

Dear God, the more I see is the more I want and need to leave the presence of wicked and evil people including spirits of this world. I more than truly love you but I truly can't take anymore wickedness and sin.

I cannot take the hatred of man anymore and I truly cannot take their wickedness.

How can we say we are going to see you when we hate each other so?

How can we say we are going to see you when we kill each other so?

How can we say we are going to see you when we have no respect of you and each other?

We have no respect for your law and laws but yet we say we are going to see you.

Tell me now, how can I save wicked and evil people if I am the saving grace for this world?

How can anyone that is of you save us knowing our evils and sins; wickedness on this earth?

How could I look my ancestors in the face and say, I forgive them that have and has hurt you so in the past and present?

How can I look you Good God in the face and say, I truly forgive them for what they have and has done to me and you; our ancestors?

How could I or can I save those who have lied to us and deceived us so if I was the saving grace of humanity? The lie took us away from you. We defiled you and cause you pain. So tell me, how can you truly save us?

How could I look at myself in the mirror knowing that I've let my people and the God that I truly love more than unconditionally down?

I truly could not nor can I. Hence I have to walk away in good faith; goodness and truth of me and you Good God. I truly love you too much to consider them when it comes to you. The disrespect is there, therefore, I cannot in good faith save any wicked and evil person including wicked and evil spirits. For me to do this would be a slap in your face Good God as well as my ancestors face and I cannot do this to you. Nor can I do this to them. I cannot save them (wicked and evil people and spirits) and condemn you. Your true love of me and my true love of thee is vital; more than important to me. The praise is due to you and to honour someone else is truly disrespectful and unfair. Therefore, I am asking you to give humanity her – the one that is to save them way before 2032. Maybe she can see the true good in humanity globally because I truly cannot with the way things are going presently globally.

I cannot stand before you and plea for anyone because I too have sinned. I too have hurt you and no amount of sorries can change this. Just like man I am flawed in regards to sin. But in all that I do, I truly have to trust and respect you. I have to give you the accolades and hope that humanity will find truth in you like I've found truth in you.

Victory is yours my king because despite it all, one did truly trust you and truly love you. So truly good luck in all that you do with humanity. I know some can be saved. But in all the saving, remember those that do to get and never ever let them into your kingdom because they have no good will; are not true to you. Never open the door to anyone wicked and evil because evil is evil and have no good will of you and your people including your natural creation; Mother Earth and Universe. In all evil did, they turned your people against you; hence never ever give them an opening anywhere ever again. Like I said Good God, I see the hatred of blacks globally and I've read the dirty comments. So how can I feel good in myself knowing the hatred of my own people? ***How can I truly save these haters if I am the saving grace of humanity. I know you never said I am the saving grace. You asked me specifically to write you a book. But how can I look to you for a saving grace for the haters of your people or my own including you if you know not them and they know not you?***

Good God, truly look at the history of man throughout the ages and see what death's people have and has done. It's not just blacks they stole from and killed. And despite me being of both lineages, how can I save any evil spirit or person no matter the race or creed? Yes, blacks have and has done evil to their own and I cannot save these people. I will never ever save them because of the evils they've done to their own. No wicked or evil will I save no matter colour, creed, race or decent.

We say we know you and or believe in you, but do all to hate and abuse you including others.

We say we know you and or believe in you, but yet kill you in all that we do including others.

We say we love you and believe in you, but as soon as someone else come along and show us their god (s) and what their god (s) can do, we jump ship and abandon you. I cannot jump ship because I know kindness and gratitude. Yes at times I want to leave you because you don't talk to me face to face like a human. You don't do all you can to make me prosperous and truly happy. You don't do all to save your people in the grand scheme of things on earth in my view. Many things I need from you but you truly don't do. Yes, I know you are not human and you cannot come into a dirty planet hence things are put in place at a point in time for me to know. Yes I thank you for this but it's not the same. At times I need to hold your hand and put my head on your shoulders and speak to you of my day and your day. Days when I am alone, feel alone and needy. Hence I am stepping aside and letting You and Death handle your own people; deal with them accordingly.

Maybe I am weird. But I need this with you. I need a perfect true and pure world with you. But how do I get this perfect true and pure world on earth when humanity have and has polluted earth with their mountainous sins and diseases including wars? Sin we cannot repay on earth. So tell me Good God, how fair is this to me and you? How is this fair to our true people that are depending on you?

I truly need fairness for me you and your people including death's people.

Good God, am I the only one that thinks this way?

Am I the only one that truly trusts you unconditionally?

Am I the only one that truly loves you more than unconditionally?

Dear God, how wonderful, good and true it would be to truly have you physically and not just spiritually. Yes I know you cannot come to man – humanity in the flesh, but why could we not see you in the rivers of your waters here on earth? Even the trees of life here on earth. I don't know, but I truly need to find you here on earth Good God. Maybe I've found you but yet I am looking for something else. Right now Good God I am tired of the hatred towards my people and you.

I am tired of looking for salvation from you and none cometh.

I am tired of the lies; your non caring attitude towards all of this; the misery on earth.

Maybe it's me, I'm the problem. Good God billions hate black people but yet their book of sin tell of his black skinned and nappy as pappy haired man (black man) that is going to save them. So if you hate the black race based on skin tone (colour), how can he; black Jesus save you? You say he's the son of God but yet Revelations say he's the son of man. So which is it? Is he the son of God or is he the son of man? I know for a fact, all of your chosen children are Black Females with one, only one being bi-racial. The brides of heaven as you call them; are all Black Females. So something is definitely wrong when it comes to the history of man and their records; history books. Like I said, you cannot change the BLACK DNA OF LIFE AND ALL. Hence the light cannot comprehend the dark; darkness. Thus white people cannot comprehend black people; the truth. Instead of embracing the truth and live in truth, you lie and kill all that is truthful without knowing when you hate and kill the truth, you are killing self; your life and own globally. Someone comes along and say hate black people because their skin is dirty you do all to kill us without truly knowing that you came from us. Everything came out of the darkness and this is truly not based on hue but based on life and death; the truth.

Yes Good God, I know that Jesus did not exist in the way man thinks he did. Jesus in truth is Black Death; meaning he is physical death. There is a Black Death and there is a White Death and I've told humanity this. The so called White Jewish translators did a horrible job of translating the truth. Meaning they could never give you the truth because they know not the truth. Jesus means Death not life because life was not given to him. Like I said, there is a Black Death and there is a White Death with White Death being the final death; the death of spirit. When we say Jesus we mean BLACK DEATH IS GOING TO TAKE OUR SPIRIT AND HAND IT OVER TO WHITE DEATH TO KILL YOU. BLACK DEATH CANNOT KILL THE TRUE YOU. IT CAN ONLY TAKE YOUR TRUE LIFE – SPIRIT AND HAND IT OVER TO WHITE DEATH FOR SENTENCING – JUDGMENT – YOUR FINAL DEATH DEPENDING ON YOUR SINS ON EARTH. Let's hope I explained that right without confusing you. So the first death you see is black death; your Black Jesus. But he does not have nappy hair. His hair is lox as in the Rasta man's hair. Female Death – Black Female Death; their hair can be lox and or braided; corn rowed. This is why I told you the Rasta's keep the order of death. And it matters not if you are White or Black Rasta. And no it matters not if you are a part of the so called Jewish race that curl their hair to look like black people. You all hold the order of death period. You cannot change this because you all have the hair on your head to prove this and or as proof. And like I said, it matters not if you cut your hair. From your name is in death's book you cannot take it out. And by you having lox – your hair locked is not a crime. You are our reminder of what death; physical death looks like.(THE HAIR). I truly love the hair hence I tell you not to cut it least life and death be truly angry at you. TRUE DEATH IS WHITE IN HUE, THE HUE OF MAN AND NOT BLACK. SO TRULY LEAVE YOUR HAIR. YOU DO NOT KILL, WHITE DEATH KILLS. AND YES WHITE DEATH LOOKS LIKE WHITE PEOPLE HENCE LIFE AND DEATH, THE YING AND YANG. And yes the Ying and Yang is true life as well. But you don't know this because you cannot comprehend life in its purest and truest form. (THE UNIVERSE).

So Black Death is the death of flesh. Meaning its Black Death and or a Black Angel that takes your spirit – sorry release your spirit from its prison the flesh. Yes there is Babylonians (Indian) death but I cannot fully tell you about them. Hence you have Christianity and Islam; the two deaths – religions of man. And even though I use Christianity and Islam as a religious reference I am wrong. Permissible yes but wrong.

Please Note:

Catholicism, Zionism in the physical form and not the spiritual form, Rastafarianism, Buddhism, Protestants, Jehovah's Witnesses, Satanists, Kabbalists, Mormons, Muslims, Scientologist, Church of God, Baptists, Anglicans, Pentecostal and whatever religion have you. You all worship and praise man. You all fall under the banner of death and it's Black Death that hands you over to White Death for your sentencing and eventual death. So if your record on earth is not clean, truly good luck to you in hell because there is no way in hell anyone is going to save you. You sinned; did wrong, hence you have to pay the penalty for your sins; wrongs. Like I've told you time and time again, IF THE LIE DID NOT WORK FOR EVE, HOW THE HELL IS THE JESUS LIE GOING TO WORK FOR YOU?

Maybe there is an opening I need to find here on earth Good God that will lead me directly to you Good God. An opening that man knows not about. Maybe I should study quantum physics in my spare time. Smile because I know quantum physics cannot get me to you. There is a portal and key in time but finding this portal and key on earth is an issue.

Yes I know I've gone too far but one day when things are not so chaotic in the world I will find you and truly live with you.

For now I have to be contented with dreams. Let's hope you will find me. Well set it in this lifetime, my physical lifetime where I find you and walk away with you in our glory, truth and perfection; cleanliness. When man is looking for me they cannot find me because I would have walked through your portal in time without shedding my flesh. Yes the portal you set in time for me and me alone to meet and join you.

Yes I am speaking about science in time but hey I am willing if you are. Just lead me truthfully to your space and time and I will be there.

Ah Good God smile because this is our day of truth. I know it's hard on you like it is on me but what can we do to resolve the lies told to man in this day and time given the time frame of man; the death of humanity before 2032.

What can we do to heal the pain of those that are going through pain and sorrow right now?

Many of us are hurt Good God, but if we cannot heal self, we have to rely on you to show us the way. We cannot hurt anymore Good God. Come on now.

Show us the way so that we do not hurt anymore.

We cannot keep begging you and you ignoring us.
We cannot keep asking but yet you leave your windows and doors closed to us.

Yes we've forgotten truth hence I am asking you to forgive us. Truly look to the kids; the children of Africa as well because they've endured enough by wicked and evil people including their own.

Good God children can learn. I know not all but why should a child suffer by the hands of wicked and evil people? This madness must stop. No child need to suffer, no child need to suffer man come on now. Look at the trouble my children give me, but I am still going. Still trying to do the best I can for them. Hence I lift my hands to you and beg you to let the hatred and war be done; go. Too many have lost their lives unnecessarily father, too many. This is life not death come on now.

Yes I know the choice we made and you cannot change this choice. We of ourselves must do this if we want and need to be saved. So please show us, each one of us how to do this; save ourselves. Hence I truly hope that you will make this madness of our sins globally end. Yes I know billions will be lost but look at the sufferation of our children and us as humans. Many have no food and many are homeless. What right does we as humans have to do this to self and them?

What right do we as humans have to hurt children; babies – ourselves?

We say we need you but yet hurt everything in sight including you.

Dear God, I know we are obligated to you and tonight with all my hurt and pain of knowing that children; black children have to suffer at the hands of human (manmade) diseases I am asking you to truly help them because what humanity – so called human beings are doing to them is truly not fair. It is wrong. ***You can't sit on the sidelines and look. Neither can she. She is the head of the spiritual church hence I am calling out to her for justice and truth also. She cannot sit and watch and do nothing to ease the pain and sufferings of these kids. She's Mother, the womb of life and she cannot ignore the pain she feels for us. Please the both of you have to do something come on now.***

Why should black children suffer and the bastards that make these diseases their family, country, people and children go free? Hence I say you are not fair

in your dealings on earth. I know I cannot blame you for any of this because we made the choice to sin and die. But you know me; I have to blame you for blaming sake. I know this is truly not fair to you but because you are my all, I give you all including the blame. This is me you know this. You are my true friend and true love. I truly have nothing to do with man but have all to do with you hence you are my true all. So subsequent to what I say, we truly cannot blame you because we made the choice to die. So however death kills us is not up to you but up death and his people – the god they choose. But I still have to come to you and plead with you for safety and justice for our people; all. Ah Good God I am but woman because the black man and woman including child have lived in ignorance and lies for far too long. Many of us know the truth but yet don't want to change our ignorance of self and this is truly a shame. We can do better but refuse to let go of the Nigger and Colonial mentality of captivity. Tell me something Good God, when did you make slaves?

When did you in all of your creating say, I am going to make slaves because we are your slaves so people should enslave each other?

When we say others are slaves; we as humans are reinforcing this lie on you. They are saying you made slaves, so therefore it is right for them to have slaves. Come on now.

I guess my dream is coming thru because you did show me black children dirty. Hence truly protect them, the children of Africa – Africans and the globe.

I know you've helped me in many things, but in truth I cannot sit and watch Africans and Africa be hurt anymore. Good God Africa is the birth place of life. So why take life from there; Africa? Yes I know you are hurt because they disobeyed you, but like I said, you have to heal. And yes we need to change and come clean. So please help us to turn from evil and clean up our dirty linen of self.

Know that I cannot sit and watch as children get hurt because wicked and evil people designed and or created diseases to eradicate another race. Good God why should one race (the black race) be eradicated to please the many that truly do not like us but hate us?

Tell me why Good God?

Did the Jamaican Motto not say, "OUT OF MANY ONE PEOPLE?" So where is your one people that is good and true Good God?

Why are we divided and not truly united in goodness and in truth in all that we do with you and self; others?

Now tell me, why are we so messed up and confused?

Why are we so vile and sinful?

Good God the devil is causing us to turn against you so he can say there, I proved you wrong. I have all your people and you are have none and you're letting him Good God and this is truly not right nor is it fair.

Good God why are we not truly united with you in all that we do?

Why do we pretend to like you by saying, "I love you God," but then turn around and praise death? Thank him for the goodness you Good God have given us.

Good God how can you sit and watch this happen?

Tell me something, how can you sit and watch the lives of a nation of people be taken from them at the hands of wicked and evil people?

How can you and her sit and watch innocent children being raped and robbed by parents and society; others?

How can you say you love us so, but yet let us continue to make the wrong choice (s) daily?

How can you say you love us so and allow all to abuse little children?

How can you say you love us so and watch Earth and the Universe die at the hands of man?

It's not just on your part Good God. People are dying, animals are being slaughtered. Tell me, what pain did these animals cause humans – humanity?

What right do these people have to murder an animal for sport?

What right does corporations – pharmaceutical companies and Laboratories have to kill and slaughter human beings and animals – life with their drugs and diseases of death at will?

What ethical right does the one and five percent have to slaughter billions for profit – their greed?

They kill at will and you let them. Hence I ask you, what part of murder is loving us so?

What right do you have to continue to permit this slaughter of life – all life?

What right?

And yes I am yelling.

Now I ask you this, WHERE IS YOUR ETHICAL RIGHTS WHEN IT COMES TO HUMAN AND SPIRITUAL LIFE; THE LIFE OF EARTH AND THE UNIVERSE?

Good God how wicked are we to do these things and how wicked are you to let these wickedness and evils continue to happen? Hence sometimes I say you are unfair despite me knowing the mandate (time of death). To me, you have no good will when it comes to true life on earth. To me you have no ethics; morals when it comes to truth, true life and cleanliness. So how can we walk with you when you have no boundaries set up for your people when it comes to life and death? Can you not say to sin and death as a god that loves us so; say death, these are my boundaries don't cross it when it comes to me and my people. They are my true love so don't overstep your right and rights. Death shouldn't cross our boundaries Good God. We shouldn't even see death's people nor allow them to come near us; much less let them come into our land and lands of goodness and truth; cleanliness. Come on Allelujah, do right by us so that we can be saved.

If you are our keep Good God and you love us so, why does sin and death infiltrate our boundaries constantly? Why not build impenetrable frameworks and foundations so that death and sin cannot come in infinitely and indefinitely forever ever without end? Yes I know I asked you this in another book, but yet you are truly not listening to me; you are ignoring me.

Tell me something, if we do not have good and solid frameworks and foundations with you, how can we live solid, good and true with anyone including you?

Look at the waterways and how we've polluted it; them.

Look at how greedy we are for all this is sinful and evil. Now look at me and tell me that you truly love me and our people in all of this; all that we do. Thought so. So if you cannot truly love, how can we?

Truly look at me and tell me that you feel my pain and hurt as to how we are living on earth.

Truly look at me and tell me that you feel my pain and hurt as to the treatment of animals on earth.

Truly look at me and tell me that you feel my pain and hurt as to the treatment of earth's waterways by humans including the trees of life and healing.

Truly look at me and tell me that you truly love life like I do. Tell me because nothing we've done on earth is fair to earth and life. Nothing we've done on earth is based on truth; true love. All is based on hate; hence we hate others and self. Come on now Good God. You know the truth but yet you've allowed evil to keep the truth from man- humanity. You allow evil to kill the truth and this is truly not right.

Tell me what is truth to you Good God and Allelujah?

Truly what is truth to you?

Yes it pains me to know what is happening on earth but as God you've let things get way too out of hand and it's not fair. You need to put earth before man in all of this because man – humanity and or humans do not respect her. Like you, they give her garbage; their mess and she has to take it and she should not have to take it. What right do we as humans have to take her life away from her?

What right do we have to rape her of everything? Hence I ask you how fair are you in life and to life?

How fair are you to earth, the trees and animals of the earth; the waterways of earth?

Now I ask you this and truly do not take it the wrong way. But where do your priorities lie when it comes to true life and the true love of earth and with us as a people?

Yes I know I have to leave wicked and evil people to time but in all you do, truly remember your people and Africa. Truly save them from the storm despite their abandonment of you. I know the uncertain future many has but I am depending on you to carry them through the storm and storms that faces them. None on earth should be the target market of death, if they are good and true; clean. Come on now Allelujah.

And truly thank you for reminding me that you will never forget your people.

Truly thank you for all because we need you to save us right now. We need you to secure our lands and people Good God and Allelujah, so that when the enemies come with their deceit and lies we are not fooled, and their lies and deceit fall back on them immediately infinitely and indefinitely forever ever without end.

Your people are not humanities scapegoat Good God, so truly look to us and supply us our need.

As I lift my hands to you, send your healing to all your African kingdoms (lands and people) and show wicked and evil people that you will never let them hurt your children and people ever again. Stand firm in your truth and true love for us and of us Good God and save our true African own.

As I lift my hands to you Good God, truly save Africa from the storms that are brewing and coming their way. Whether those storms be financial, diseases created and manufactured by men; wicked and evil people to kill them (Africans and their African lands) you need to help Africa and her people. Good God it matters not if these storms are physical or spiritual. You truly need to help Africa and her people weather them. Not for me but for you and them (Africa and Africans). You need to help them because I cannot take the hurt and pain anymore. It's October 21, 2014 and I read that WHO (World Health Organization) is doing a clinical test on a vaccine to help Africa.

Good God a clinical test of an Ebola drug!!!!!!!!!!!!!!!!!

Good God are Africans guinea pigs?

Good God and Allelujah, who the hell is WHO (World Health Organization)?

Bleep them with their deadly drugs. A vaccine is readily available in the United States for Ebola. Why not give Africa this drug to help their people? But like everything else a new drug and vaccine will be issued to Africa and before long a new form a disease will hit them; the land and people of Africa. And the propaganda ring of evil and deceit; lies will begin all over again for Africa and her African people. Why spend so much money to create and manufacture a new vaccine when a vaccine already exist? This does not make any sense whatsoever.

You the World Health Organization do not work in the behalf of anyone. You work in the behalf of extinction; the eradication of human and animal life – all life forms. So truly bleep your lying asses and your shit – murderous vaccine that you will give to Africa to now further infect African people and Africa with. Hence I am asking you Good God not to let their murderous tendencies and lies and deceit go unnoticed. There is judgment to be declared Good God and I am declaring this Judgment as of this day October 21, 2014. Allelujah, glory be to you Good God, glory to your name. Judgment, Judgment, Judgment. Let thy true and good will be done Good God unto the World Health Organization and the countries and people that are affiliated with them. Truly turn from WHO (the World Health Organization) because they are liars and deceivers. Truly save Africa and the animals of Africa. Yes the African people need to be punished for letting people come into Africa and murder the animals for sport. For this I will not ask penance for the people and governments of Africa that allow this. They need to be punished because they the African people allow this. So whatever punishment you so give; declare unto to Africans not the land of Africa for letting people hunt the animals of Africa to extinction and the brink of extinction I will concede to. I will not argue with you for this. Africa is for Africans; you and the people of Africa have and has deceived you whilst causing you hurt and pain; shame and disgrace. I will not curse you for because Africans know better but yet refuse to do better. So yes vindicate the animals of Africa according to your laws of truth. They; the animals belong to you also hence they have life. No one should kill an animal for sport. I will not tolerate this because no animal wage war against man. Humanity is the one to wage war against animals, hence hunting them to extinction to suit their evil own; murderous and wicked tendencies of self.

Good God you said you will never forget us, hence prioritize the life of your people; our people. Put us first in all that you do in goodness and in truth. Africa has always been the first and the last. Hence let the destruction of Africa and her people stop now. Punish their evils, but stay the destruction of African lands for our mercies and thy mercies sake. We as blacks need you, so help us to come clean and come back truthfully to you. Africa is the birthplace of life. It is also the hub of life and the universe and you can no longer let Africa and her people be destroyed. Also, you cannot let the people of Africa destroy you. You are the creator of all including this earth and universe.

Africa has always been the Alpha and the Omega but yet you neglect her and she neglects you. How can you never forget us and love us so if everyone is killing Africa and her people; the true black race? This isn't love Good God; this is hatred on your part. Whites and Blacks lived in peace and harmony; truth long before the Babylonians came along and now look at us? Destitute and fighting amongst and against our own; each other.

Africans were the first to be lied to. They were the first to be destroyed (people). Now we are at the end; last of days and the destruction of Satan's children and people has come full throttle to Africa in the form of diseases, Genetically Modified Foods (GMO foods) and financial and economic drain. Hence I ask you, when does it stop? When did you turn into death? When did you forget where your priorities lie when it comes to life – good and true life all around?

You cannot say you love us so and watch others kill your people. There is no just cause for death; murder. You cannot continue to neglect your own. Hence I ask you again, where are your priorities when it comes to your people; good and true life on a whole? Where do you truly stand with us? Come on now. You cannot say we are neglectful and stiff necked when you are the same. Death has time yes. Yes I know we created the time of death, but you of yourself know that death could be stopped; can be stopped but yet you refuse to help us stop it; death. Remember you showed me the Jewish man that had the power to cause evil to flee (Islam). You also showed me the Black Man that could separate the lands. Remember the phone number the Jewish man gave me if I needed to contact you. So why isn't this phone number working?

Why can't I get through to you?

Did you change your number?

So now tell me, with all that is happening, where is your truth in all of this; all that you do?

Where is your truth of your people?

You created it all but yet you are watching it being destroyed by wicked and evil people; humans that have not your best interest at heart.

Why create life then?

Why let others; the ones that were formed from the dust of the earth destroy it all?

What sense does it make Good God?

Good and evil cannot coexist in peace, so truly let evil go. Let the final separation begin and begin now. Thus saith the Lord thy God. Do not further the flames of evil anymore come on now.

Yes I know the course of death and death must take his and her people but open the eyes of your people (black people not based and hue) and let them see that the way they are following is the way of death. Open their eyes and let them see that it's their sins of believing and following other gods that is doing this to them.

<u>Good God let us change our course of destruction. We need to get on your good and true road to life and we cannot do this in an unclean state. We must become clean, hence truly lead the way to you in goodness and in truth; honesty.</u>

Other gods mean them (Africa and your people) no good. We are dying because this is what the god and gods they give us to serve want. Their god is not higher than life, hence we (your children and people) must change our dirty linen of self; ways and come clean so that we will be saved indefinitely.

Good God you gave my homeland a saying grace hence truly give Africa a saving grace but only your true people. I know Babylonians live in Africa and I will never open the door for any of them; any Babylonian out of true respect of you. *<u>If they truly love you let them find you on their own accord.</u>*

Good God, I cannot beg you for any Babylonian because in all I do, I also think of your hurt and pain, my ancestors hurt and pain. They the Babylonians lied to my ancestors and it caused them their place with you. So why should I think of them or even try to save any Babylonian in all that I do? I have to think of your hurt and pain and the cost to you; your people. I have to respect you in all that I do. Hence I refuse to comply with the lies and religions of men and women including spirits in the spiritual and physical realm. I also refuse to comply with the lies and deceit on men anywhere on earth and in the universe.

You are life Good God and we have to live life good and true. Like I've said, you are our right and you are life. You are our lifeline and hope. So truly stop being the scapegoat for death and his lying and deceiving people. Judgment has been passed, so truly let the judgment stay. You cannot live to kill because life is precious whether human or animal, tree or water including air; the atmosphere and universe.

Good God, I saw on the internet where these people slaughtered an animal in Africa for sport. Wow. Good God, they had the American flag on the animal they slaughtered and you are going to let this go unnoticed?

Good God ban Americans and punish them; punish everyone globally that use African animals for sport infinitely and indefinitely forever ever without end. Come on now. *<u>Like I said,</u>*

**punish the African people for letting evil and wicked people come into Africa to hunt the animals of Africa for sport and money. Punish the people of African lands including governments that allow people to come into Africa and slaughter animals to extinction and near extinction.** And like I said, you need to know where your priorities lie when it comes to life – good and true life all around because humans have not a heart when it comes to life; good and true life period.

And Good God in all of this and my ranting of you, truly thank you for liking and truly loving me. Please forgive me where I go wrong. Hold me close to you in all I do because I do truly love you unconditionally.

Michelle Jean

In all we know Good God humanity still do not have the full truth. They are still lost because the black race is still clueless as to why the book of sin was written.

Wow Good God because we still do not know that every black man woman and child must die and it matters not where we live.

King Herod gave the commission to his people to kill us all – every Jewish child – the savior – humanities so called savior. But King Herod did not want to kill the savior, he could not. He wanted to kill the black race hence many were slaughtered; killed. King Herod knew that he could not get into your kingdom and or abode Good God, so because of this, black people must be killed; slaughtered at will.

King Herod knew what he was doing. Kill us (the entire black race), take their land and lands; change history – our history, the black man's history to reflect them. Give us White hope and spread death; White death and lies.

Yes all must be taken from the black race including African lands; our African homes. All he did worked but what he did not tell his people was that the more they kill, is the more they die; lock themselves out of truth; your good and true kingdoms and abode Good God and Allelujah. He forgot to tell them, the more they kill and steal, is the longer they stay in hell and burn before their eventual death; extinction.

Good God man's so called holy book is their book of death. All who believe in this book will never see you; cannot be saved. All they do is for death, therefore, death is their god. Death is whom they believe in. Death is the one carrying them through not life. Hence death is the one to kill them and take them home to hell.

<u>Yes Satan won against man. Satan wasn't looking for money he was looking for your souls. The agenda of death has always been death no matter the hue; colour.</u>

Death had to keep hell going and in order to keep hell going was to cause you to sin reckless and rude whilst having you believing in a savior that's going to save you. You had to sin and you did sin, hence signing a contract with death and sealing your fate; soul and or spirit in hell. Hence you sould (sold) your soul.

Satan and or Death knew that certain sins were automatic death and no matter how much good you do, you cannot be saved. Hence billions of you will stay in hell for trillions of years depending on the severity of your sins and or how much sin is on your plate of sin and or written in your record of sin and sins.

Like I've said, if the lie did not work for Eve (Evening), how is the Jesus lie going to work for you?

You sinned but yet expecting someone else to pay the price for you with his or her life. We say we are educated but yet the devil has us all fooled. So if we live like fools how can we say we are educated; wise?

Oh well such is life I guess. Life is different because as we cannot see our insides. Hence we cannot see our spirit.

Weird by true.

Our lives are different hence each one of us is different in the physical and spiritual world.

Michelle Jean

Oh Good God if only I could wake up one day and see a different moon and sun – world.

If only I could wake up and see all evil and wickedness gone from Earth infinitely and indefinitely forever ever without end.

Ah Good God how joyous it would be to hold your hand and say thank father well done.

Ah Good God If only this could be my good and true reality where I truly do not have to see physical and spiritual wickedness anymore because all that is wicked and evil would be gone indefinitely.

Good God, how good and wonderful it would be to have no evil just pure honest clean positive and true energy that's good and true, honest and clean all the time.

Maybe I live in a fantasy world of hoping and talking to you Good God, but this is our world that is pure and true, truly honest good; clean.

Good God is it wrong to ask you of this and or for this?

Is it wrong to need all that is good and true, clean and righteous here on earth and in the spiritual realm?

Dear God there would be no more death. All would be good and clean; true.

Maybe now with all this, Earth can grow – expand in goodness and in truth; greatness.

Maybe now with all of this Earth can be truly free to do her; what she truly needs to do void of all evil and wickedness; sin.

Good God, do you not want and need all these beautiful things too?

Do you not desire truth and true goodness like me?

Do you not yearn for all that is good and true; clean like me?

Do you not desire and yearn cleanliness like me Good God and Allelujah?

Ah Good God, if only you could see what I see? What I need for Earth and humanity; all life including you.

Ah Lovey, if only, truly if only.

If I could create wholesome and true, void of all sin and evil, I would just to give it to you.

Ah Lovey, you truly don't know me, hence if only, truly if only.

Michelle Jean

Ah Good God why can't you truly know me?

No wait, I truly don't want or need to start this with you. I need nature, need to see nature and be with nature. Yes nature is my natural high, natural sex and sex toy.

I can dance with nature; play with nature because nature is all around me. Well not the way I need it to be. But Good God, how wonderful it is to just wake up and see everything green and beautiful; all green trees and not the dead and or hibernating ones.

Good God can you see me?

Moi, I just kissed you on the cheek.

Yes it's crazy me, but I so wanted to do that. Well at that moment anyway.

See Good God you've consumed my thoughts, hence I truly need to do something different for me.

No we can't go to dinner. Don't want to walk into a restaurant by myself. Need to walk in hand in hand and clearly with you.

Is that even possible Good God given the vanity trend?

We don't marry to stay together nor do we get together to stay together. Relationships are just fronts; the who I am seen with on a given day.

God you truly have to wonder if these people can stand each other.

Dear God I truly don't know with humans now a days.

Good God, why do you stay away from me? I mean, why do I not see you each and every day?

Good God, you are my true love. But yet I can't see you and talk to you face to face daily in this relationship in the physical and spiritual. Tell me, are you ugly and that's why you are hiding from me?

No that can't be it. You are definitely not ugly but hey I got to be human.

Smile.

Hey here's my happy face with you.

Can't burst out laughing lest my kids think I am crazy.

Good God for me stay real. You are cool even if you don't let me see you face to face to truly hug you and tell you thanks for being there for me.

Maybe one day when all is well between me and you and the earth we can walk and talk hand in hand. And yes man oh man am I ever going to pinch you.

Woo Nelly you be mine now.

Yes I know you are the father but that don't mean I can't pinch you. Nope you can't hide from me now because I will find you hence my word search.

Michelle Jean
October 15, 2014

Ah Good God I need you right away. Mood changing, no not mood changing just lonely nights and days.

Night fall. Oh man if only I could jump to another universe and avoid these long nights. As soon as it gets night fall where I'm at, then I would jump back to the daylight.

Good God winter nights are lonely if you are by yourself. Maybe it's the fact that I want to escape this life and go somewhere where I can meditate without the stress and noise.

Yes I would turn all my phones off. Better yet who needs a phone?

Yes I am crazy but I truly don't want to be amongst anyone right now.

Need me some solitude. Good God and Michelle time.

Is there such a thing though God?
Is there a Good God and Michelle time?

If there is, can it be all the time? Come on don't say no. I know, I know the universe and all the other lives that reside with you as well as, those who are slated to join you and those who are depending on you. But in truth, can't there be a Michelle and Good God time all the time?

I know, I know, I do not have the monopoly on you but why not? Why can't I monopolize you? Why can I have you all to myself all the time?

I want to be the one and only special one in your life.

Yes this is sad and greedy on my part when it comes to you, but hey this is me on my crazy days sometimes.

Pity

Well no not pity because it would be unfair to all if I monopolize you. Got to be just and true hence I have to be fair. But with all that said, if I could I would just to have me some Michelle and Good God Time. Hey Good God, couldn't you just do this for me and only me. Have special times where you and I go out for walks? Maybe coffee or tea. You do the buying though because I want to be spoiled by you.

Michelle Jean
October 15, 2014

Am I crazy?

Good God do you think I'm crazy? No don't answer that. Everyone in your abode think I am wacked. Truly love you too much. Smile.

But for real Good God do they?

Am I the wacked out one that tells you everything?

No don't answer that. I am, hence I see you smiling and enjoying my crazy words.

But Good God, what is life if we can't truly smile?

What is life if we can't truly be ourselves with you?

Ah well Good God, I truly hope you don't think you made a mistake in asking me to write you a book.

Yes I've written many under the Michelle Jean banner and I do hope you read them. Yes they have many mistakes due to the fact that I do not have an editor. And yes I know I can't have one because you called me and me alone to write you a book. Mistakes are plenty but I did do my best to catch all the mistakes and you know this. Sometimes I don't want to and I've let many books go but that is my spirit. It's not easy writing for you Good God because I write like I speak and spell like I speak; hence dictionaries I truly do not use. Do not want or need to be politically correct by man's standard. As long as I am correct, just and true by you and your standards in all that I do that's all that matters to me. I am not here to convince anyone to accept you because like I've told you, we are to know you and be true and right to you and by you. We know better hence we are to do better. We cannot say we love you then turn around and hurt you. That's not love that's hate. Hence I say it's the ones that say they love you that mess up and screw up your life royally.

Some mess up your life to the point of you going into the psyche ward. Some commit suicide. But in all that we do, we hurt, hence true love is rare and cannot hurt in any way or form. True love governs good and true life, hence true love cannot be found in all humans.

True love is unconditional and free and this is what I truly have for you Good God. So truly smile and enjoy the rest of your day; evening. And yes I dedicate LIVE ON by Beres Hammond and Marcia Griffith to you.

Michelle Jean
October 15 and 22, 2014
December 07, 2014

Good God, are you as crazy as me sometimes?

Do you yearn to be happy like me?

Do you yearn to go places but can't, just like me?

Do you yearn and desire true love just like me?

So Good God, why can't we pool our resources together in truth and honesty and create a clean and true place where we can go? Just me and you and your true and good people.

I mean earth is dirty by our standards, yours and my standard due to sin; the sins of man – humanity. So why can't we find a clean, true and good place where we can go? We can create one out of the waters all around if we can't find a good true and clean place to go here on earth.

Good God there is so much that I truly need to be educated on, so why can't we find that truly good and clean place where you can truly educate me? I truly do not need bits or pieces from dreams where I have to figure things out. I need truth, the full truth without the figuring out and searching, wondering and hoping.

Ah Good God all I can do is yearn; wish and think about you and this good and true place of peace that is void of all evil and sin including void of all spiritual evils and sin.

For now I guess I will stay day dreaming of this good and true, clean and truly peaceful and harmonious place where the both of us can meet; join.

Michelle Jean
October 15 and 22, 2014

Good God, you see all that is happening on earth with humanity in regards to the creating and distributing of diseases – biological, genetic and germ warfare.

Now I ask you this. These people that design create and implement these killing agents and machines. How do they sleep at nights knowing that they kill people daily with their manmade diseases, germs and war machines?

How do they sleep knowing that they are going to burn in hell for hundreds of trillions of years before their final extinction?

Good God, how do you look at them and their families including ancestors?
How do you even look at man knowing the ills and sins we have done?

How do you live with yourself knowing just how vile, wicked and evil we as humans have become?

Good God, I don't know anymore because none of this makes any sense. Why kill to go to hell?

Why give your life unto death when you know you are going to burn in hell; die?

Father, I truly don't know what to say. Yes I am sick but I try to keep going and complain to you but why kill yourself for death? Why not live for life and live?

You know what Good God maybe it's not for me to know. Maybe I am the insane one. But why Good God? Why live to die when you gave us good and true life to live by?

Hell is not your good and clean abode, so why would humans want to go to hell and face the fires and torment of hell? Do they not know about demons; the demons of hell?

Ah Good God, I cannot think anymore because my head will start to hurt if I continue thinking.

So for now I'd better leave death and his children alone. I cannot ask why anymore because we all make choices and we have to live by those choices; the choices we made and make.

Life is better than death but yet we choose death anyway.

Michelle Jean
October 17 and 22, 2014

Ah Good God come away to the Blue Mountain with me.

Let's watch the stars together
Spend a night or two
Just you and me talking; reminiscing

We could share a glass of wine or two
But truly meet me there so that I can talk to you.

Dear God let all my dreams come through in a good and clean way.

Yes you can bless me beyond measure in all that is good and clean; positive and honest; truly prosperous and true.

Good God, share with me your world so I can live it clean and void of all obstacles and sins more than infinitely and indefinitely forever ever without end.

Good God, truly make Blue Mountain a reality for me and you if it be thy will.

Ah Good God. If only you weren't a fantasy. Well at times I feel as if you are a fantasy. At times I just want to shout and say see me. I am right here. Why pick me if you are going to ignore and neglect me; hinder me?

Why pick me if you are going to leave me stranded; all alone?

What sense does it make to pick someone but yet leave them in sin; poverty?

This is crazy Good God, but yet I feel this way.

Yes it's crazy but this is my life and I have to live it I guess.

Oh well such is life when it comes to you and me. But meet me on the Blue Mountain. Let us converse; have fun; truly talk; walk.

Dear God show me the way and truly do not disappoint me in my asking.

Truly come away with me to the Blue Mountain. Let us relax and sleep. Let me see you and talk to you. We truly need to talk because the people of earth is in a bad state and we need to fix this problem before it is truly too late for your people; you and me.

Michelle Jean
October 17 and 22, 2014

Ah God what a day. Yeah the heart monitor is gone. Yeah me but my heart is lonely.

Good God, in all I see and view when it comes to living on earth is that I truly do not want or need to live in concrete jungles nor do I continuously want to be so lonely. I truly do not want to live in noise and sin, nor do I want to live amongst wicked and evil people. Yes I am lonely because I am one. One is damned lonely hence I truly do not want nor do I need to be single anymore. Yes I feel like Adam when it comes to loneliness; but truly don't send me any Eve's or Evil's; Sin of wickedness and evil to come and comfort me. I more than infinitely and indefinitely need truth and truthful people. So truth all the way even if it is in the one. The one and only you send me. No that's not right, I need the one you send me to be fully and truly truthful, honest, caring, truly love nature, truly good and positive, clean and responsible; mature. All that is around me and surrounds me must be good and true, clean and righteous all the time indefinitely.

Good God, when I see cities, tall buildings they truly scare me. Is this what life has truly become?

Good God, I need you but in truth I cannot live in the city nor can I build you your mega mansion that I've put on hold in the city.

Good God, I truly cannot give you a city dwelling because in all honesty, I truly would not come and visit you. The city offers me nothing and I am scared, truly scared of the city. So why would I live in the city or even build you anything in the city.

Good God, I loathe the city more than passionately. I can't wait to leave the city I am in but yet I am stranded here.

Ah Good God could I give you a mountain view with a country side mansion? A view cut off from the city and others; concrete jungles.

Good God a countryside estate with a mega mansion suits us. Yes hopefully we could have over a hundred million acres of land for us and our people here on earth.

Good God this place must have lots of trees and fruit trees. Yes we will plant some of our own too.

Where we live Good God must be secluded and private. No one can find us because I would truly have you; truly have the Breath of Life. No one can come near us because we would be all we need. Good God, we could have everything but you know me; sometimes I have to nag. Yes you would be my tight – overly tight and extremely protective security.

Dear God, could we not start the road to recovery as of January 2015 where I will find that piece of land that is private, clean, right and suitable for us where no planes can fly over including drones?

Good God why can't this be? Why can't we truly find each other in true peace and harmony?

Michelle Jean
October 17 and 22, 2014

Ah Good God it's Friday night and I so need my own place and privacy. I need to sprawl out in my own bed.

I need to be naked in my own room.

Good God, I need to be free to do the nasty.

Need to be free to nag you; somebody.

Yes I am lonely and I truly don't want to be anymore. But yet you can't understand this nor can you comprehend my loneliness. You want and need me to be lonely hence the lonely thoughts in some of these books.

Tell me something Good God, why the hell do you want to keep us lonely and depressed?

Why should anyone live their life lonely?

Is loneliness not death to you like it is to me? So if loneliness is death and confusion, why do you keep your people; me specifically lonely?

Why do you keep us lonely whilst we keep looking for you and needing you?

Are you lonely Good God hence you have to keep me at least so lonely?

Why do I have to be lonely Good God?

Why does everything take so long with you when it comes to me and you?

Why can't things be easy for me when it comes to you and all that I do that is good and true for you and me; us?

Why can't my prosperity come easily?

Tell me the truth. You don't want me to have a mate do you?

You know what Good God; I am going to leave this confusion and yoyo emotions alone for another day.

Can't do the loneliness crap anymore.

So Good God, are you going to join me in the Blue Mountain real soon?

Are you going to make me meet Mr. Right up there?

No that's not you. You allow the wrong ones to come my way. Hence let me leave well enough alone. Just for once, I truly wish you could do right and just by me. But then again this isn't truly you.

Sometimes you leave me hanging. Oh well this is you I guess. This is our life of me doing all the writing and talking to you and for you.

For once can't you do for me Good God? But in all your doing, do not let anyone take me and my true love from you.

Why are you so damned lazy when it comes to me?

It's like, just leave it, Michelle will find it; find the truth.

Why can't I rely on you for my true goodness? Like I said, you are a great protector but a lousy teacher and provider.

For once do for me clearly and out of goodness and kindness for me and you. I know what you need at times and I am trying for you, but why can't you try in goodness for me? Do for me so that I can continue to do for you.

Yes make me feel important. I am not a slave nor am I your slave. So truly don't make me feel like one. I do not do this to you, so why the hell should you hurt me like this? This isn't loving so, this is hatred. Stringing me along for a long and tedious ride that leaves me yearning, wanting and needy; lonely is not just nor is it fair to me.

Just once can you do something truly nice and special for me? Something that is from you to me in goodness and in truth.

Michelle Jean
October 17 and 22, 2014

Good God, what the hell is going on between me and you?

I asked you to come away with me and you keep showing me dry trees.

Good God, don't piss me off now.

Remember I gave you flowers and you made them wither and die. I did not make them wither and die, you did. I gave you those flowers out of goodness and truth; true love and you killed them not me. Now I ask you to come away with me and you are showing me trees that have no life. So are you saying if I go on this vacation I am dead to you? Well so be it because I am sick and tired of you killing the trees; life.

I am sick and tired of you going up against me. I am not dead and you can't kill me.

I am going away whether you like it or not and I refuse to allow you to hinder me. You don't tell me where I can go to make you and me happy so you are at fault not me. I came to you truthfully and clean in regards to this vacation and you are saying no.

I am not the dry one you are. Hence I have to bring her back in the picture where she said God kills. You kill our hopes and dreams.

You shelter our lives and expect us to be okay when you take all from us.

You are not fair, you are evil. I've listened to you about Jamaica but I will not listen to you about Blue Mountain. I am going and if this means the end of me and you so be it. I don't need drought, I need life and you are obviously not it. I am tired of the separation now and I am tired of the damned loneliness. I do not live in freaking hell so why are you keeping me in hell? Come on now.

You want to be lonely then bleeping stay lonely but don't bring me down with you with your damned negative energy and loneliness. Keep your damned negativity to yourself. I need positivity, positive energy and truth around me at all times. You are not clean nor are you honest when you keep us lonely. You want us to die and I refuse to die with you. Keep doing you and I will now start to do me.

No man, I am tired of you not being truly true to me. Tell me, who wouldn't be fed up of your bullshit? Why hinder me now at this the final stage of life?

Yes I went up Bull Head Mountain and I need to fix this mountain up but my homeland is unclean so I cannot fix it up. If this is not the right mountain (Blue Mountain) then say so clearly but don't dry up the trees; everything because I am sick of it.
Who the hell are you to dry up the trees?

How dare you? And yes I am angry. Stop showing me dead trees because you know how I am when it comes to life; trees. So because you dried up those beautiful trees you had better plant 3 not 2, but 3 for each one you dried up. And you had better plant good and true trees too including fruit trees with good and positive; clean and honest roots. I will not have you hurting and or harming the trees because they did you nothing. And don't you dare smile down at me saying that's my girl. Hot headed and bold face. You do not show me the right direction to go in but yet you are expecting me to do right and true by you. Tell me something Good God, what did the trees do to you for you to be drying them up so?

You are cruel and wicked; unjust and unfair to the trees. How dare you cause them to die?

You could have said, Michelle I do not want you to go on this trip but noooooooooooooo you could not do that. You had to take it out on the trees. Well shame on you and yes the poor trees.

__Don't you ever do that again to the trees because this is between me and you and you have no right doing this to them; the trees. How would you like it if I withered something that was of importance to you?__

Remember, you are the one to refuse to talk.

You're the one to keep your mouth shut.

You are the one to keep us hanging and when we want to do something for self and you, you stop us. Well I am fed up of you now.

I am fed up of you taking away from my dreams and true happiness.

No wonder we fail you in all that we do. You constantly fail us. You know how I am when it comes to life – the beauty of trees and here you are like a big jerk withering them and killing them. I truly love you and all but do not touch my trees. I will cuss you out brutal for the trees.

So truly don't do it again because the trees of life did you nothing and I refuse to let you harm and or hurt them. Grow up and prioritize your damned self; life.

You are God and Life but you do not act like Good God and Good Life. There are issues on earth and you cannot run away from these issues. These issues need to be solved; addressed and we as humans cannot do it by ourselves. You left us alone for billions of years and throughout history look at what we've done to self. The alone business is not working because man cannot bring themselves to learn the truth. You have the key to truth; so stop death and the lies that are given to us. This is the final seconds of man not minutes and you have the key to save your good and true people; so truly save them. Let us be rid of all sin and evil so that we can live. The spirit can be changed, but we cannot just do this in the spiritual. We must do this change in the physical as well.

And don't say it because I am not petitioning you for death and or sins wicked and evil people, I am petitioning you for your good and true people. You cannot leave us hanging and think that we are going to be okay because we are not going to be okay and you know this.

You cannot ask me to write and not expect me to be truthful to you in all that I do. Like I said, true love is rare and if you find true love, cherish it and nurture it so that it can grow. Do not kill me and the good and true life you have given me. Do not kill us and make me die because at the end of the day, you are going to cry and live in regret. Just as I nurture you all around nurture me also. Come on now.

Life is worth it and I am still going on my trip whether you like it or not. Maybe not now or ever but on this day because of you withering the trees and letting them look dry as if they are dead; you are a big jerk in my book just for today and yes because of the trees. You owe me a vacation not that you could afford one. Jerk. How dare you take your disapproval out on the trees? You cannot kill the trees. Trees are life, so why hurt them?

Dummy and Jerk because I am cussing you for the trees. Touch not my trees. And yes I am sorry for cussing you but my gorgeous and beautiful trees no one touch – harm or kill not even me; you.

Michelle Jean

Good God, you know me but you have to do better when it comes to me and you.

You know what, forget it because I'm just going to get pissed off if I continue to write and think because you are unjust and unfair. Hence I have to wonder if it's death I've been dealing with all along.

I have to wonder, truly wonder about you. Everything hath life Good God and I can't deduce anymore.

I truly cannot live by your constraints and restrictions anymore. If you are not willing to live truthful and clean, how can I be with you? How can anyone live truthfully and clean with you if you are not clean?

The trees did you nothing but yet you dried them up. Good God that one tree has many leaves and if you dry up the trees then the leaves are dried up also; dead. So what gives you the right to do this? ***KNOW THAT THE ONE DOES AFFECT THE MANY.***

SO IF YOU DRY YOURSELF UP, ARE YOU NOT TAKING FROM THE MANY GLOBALLY?

ARE YOU NOT DRYING UP US ALSO?

Are you not killing us?

Yes I am questioning your authority and integrity and I am sorry to do this, but I have to on this day. Yes the trees.

When you kill a tree all dies with that tree. So why do it?

We all have a tree of life Good God, but you cannot see this goodness.

To me it matters not to you and I am tired of it. The loss of one good tree takes the lives of many with it and you know this. That tree also signifies human life, so when you kill one good tree like you did in my dream, then you kill many in life and this is not right.

You have an obligation to life whether you like it or not. Yes we have sinned as humans and this affect our spiritual life, hence our leaf fall off the tree of life. But with me wanting to go to Blue Mountain should not have caused you to wither and or dry up the trees. Yes I know life and you are showing me what is wrong from what is right, but truly leave the Trees of Life alone. Truly do not let my sins affect the many because it is truly not fair to them. They are not the ones that need this vacation I am. So truly protect them; our good and true people from my sins.

Truly look at the leaves on that one tree Good God. So truly think about what you are doing. Look at how many trees humans have and has cut down without truly planting back more for what for they have taken; killed. What are you doing about these people and or corporations? But yet I want to go to Blue Mountain with you and all you can do is show me dried and or withered up and or dead trees. You don't do anything for them (the trees that have been cut down globally) but you want to cut me down because of my desire.

Wow, how unfair and unjust are you?

Like I've said, if I am the saving grace for humanity, I will not save any wicked and evil person or spirit and now this includes you Good God and Allelujah because I see where you are not just nor are you fair and true. So truly know where your priorities lie when it comes to good and true people; goodness and truth; cleanliness – people that truly love and care for you including the trees; environment on a whole.

I've told you about concrete jungles how I despise and detest them. Like I said, I refuse to build you your home; house in any concrete jungles. I tell you this clearly but yet you are truly not clear and true with me.

Like I said, I truly love you but you have to truly do better when it comes to me and you and yes the trees; environment globally.

Am I the rational one in all of this?

Am I the one to see the bigger picture and greater good in all of this; when it comes to the goodness of me and our people the trees and environment on a whole?

I don't know but you have to do better. You have to let your evil side go if you have one and truly care about me; us; your good and true people on a whole.

Michelle Jean

Good God you know that I am tired, so why is it that you can't let me achieve my goals – destiny; dreams?

I don't know today because the directions I take is wrong when it comes to me and you and I am truly fed up of it.

Truly fed up of the bullshit life with you.

If you don't direct us in the right direction, will we not be continuously lost?
Will we not continuously go in the wrong direction?

We won't be able to find you. Is this what you truly want?

Yes I am running from it all because I truly need to be away from it all; the madness and wickedness of people in this world. Maybe this is what you did and in truth I truly don't blame you. The killings of man and the sins of man do affect you; your spirit and all.

I can't stay with you anymore either. Hence I am stepping aside as of 2015 January 1.

I can't deal with you and your lies anymore, so truly do you and Death can do them.

You don't touch the trees like that man come on now. What did they do to you?

What have the trees done to you?

You cannot kill life but here you are taking life and killing life – the trees in my dream.

So she was not wrong when she said God kills.

But why?

If you are disappointed tell the person clearly you are disappointed because I know you can, but yet you keep your mouth shut. I get it, I get it, but I am tired and I can't take the pressure no more. If you do not open good doors for me or anyone to go in, how can I or anyone be pleased with you? How can anyone go in or through these good doors if you do not open them for us?

If you don't see my greater good that I have for you, my children, me and our family, how can I trust you or even want to reside with you?

Look at it Good God. I truly cannot see the beauty in concrete jungles. Building here there and everywhere and I've told you this. I see the beauty in trees – nature, hence I truly do not like the autumn and winter months because they take away life from me and you.

I truly love all that is green and true around me. So truly stop hurting the trees. Yes I know we need Autumn and Winter but I truly don't need these months. Hence I need to go away to a place that is warm for the Autumn and Winter Months. Yes I will return in the spring and summer months. Is that so hard for you to do for me? Is this so hard for you to understand; comprehend.

Trees represent life, human life. So when you make them die, you make us as humans die also. Yes I know the significance of the dream. Hence I have to be true to life; you. I also have to be true to the seeds you have and has given me. I cannot go to the Blue Mountain, at least not this one anyway. If I go then I would have failed you and the people you have given me. So yes mi wi kip mi ass quiet for them, me and you.

Talk to me not hurt the trees. I need them (the trees) so truly don't do it again. It's not necessary because trees have roots with you and mother earth. Plus they grow up to you in goodness and in truth.

A man's life can be seen and read in the life of a tree and a tree leaf depending on his or her tree of life. So truly no more hurting the trees; trees of life – humans.

These trees were tall and big (fat) and you know me on fat things. So truly leave my good and true babies – the trees alone.

Thank you.

And please note, I did not set out to disrespect you nor am I disrespecting you Good God. There is a special place in my heart for trees and it irks me when I look around and not see many trees. We take from the trees of life as humans and do not plant back the proper amount to replace the one tree we've taken. So tell me, how can life be the same when we as humans take all from life all around?

You are Good God and the God of all, so you truly need to be fair and just in all that you do.

I know the harvest comes and this cannot be helped. Like I said, we are the ones to make the choice to die and I cannot be like everyone. I need to live; hence I call on good life to save what truly belongs to good and true life. The trees and waterways belong to life hence we must save them Good God. We cannot neglect good and true life. We cannot neglect earth. She needs you because you did give her us to sustain and maintain us for a time.

So Good God, truly thank you once again for all and truly thank you for taking the blunt of my cussing in all these books. I truly need to wake up to you – the trees of life and I cannot have you or anyone destroying them. As humans we can do better hence I am calling out to you as well as crying out to you for good and true help; life.

Michelle Jean
October 18 and 22, 2014

As I come to a close with this book Good God, I will not use my other ending. Like I said, you have to know where your priorities lie. We are down to the final seconds of life in spiritual years and you cannot under any circumstances let your people be caught up in the mess that is going to unfold shortly on earth.

It's no longer rumors of war, it is war. Look at Sudan and all the African nations. Look at earth globally and see the mess we have caused and done. My homeland was deemed unclean by you. I was told recently Japan and Jamaica is going to be destroyed but I cannot cry. Like I said, when he (the white gentleman) told me this I was like Sarah in the living. I laughed. I cannot cry for my own anymore because we caused this on self.

We neglected the truth.

We neglected you and accepted lies.

We ignored your messengers and now it's too late for the people and the island. All I can do now is watch and wait. But when it happens (destructions come) Good God, I truly don't want anyone to find me. I need to be at peace with this because I refuse to stop death. Death wanted Jamaica and they were stopped twice, but this time around death stays. Meaning death must take his and her own. I refuse to stand in death's way because I know just how deadly female death is and can be. Like I said, Good God, I can blame you because I've made you my all and best friend. But I will not allow you to hurt the trees because the trees of life did you nothing. No I am not breaking you down because I made sure I have more than impenetrable foundations and frameworks with you.

The only breaking down to be done is you breaking down. You breaking me down and I refuse to let you continue to do this to me. I will not break down because I know just how evil evil is and I refuse all facet of evil whether physical or spiritual; universal.

We all have issues yes, but those issues we made not you Good God. It's just like Eve in Evil's so called beginning. She had you and because she did not listen to you she got cast out of your abode infinitely and indefinitely. I cannot be like her nor can I live like her. One tree affects the many like I've said and I cannot allow myself to lose you or the many. I cannot allow myself to lay careless and let your people; your true people lose their place with you. Yes I go ballistic on you but this is me. I know you are trying to protect us including me and I thank you for this. The tree dream just mean if I go to the Blue Mountain now, I would be taking away from the lives of the many you have and has given me. I know this; hence I have to do better to protect myself and them; your true people and you. Our trees of life.**

So for my rudeness and anger truly forgive me but like I said, I truly need to be away from all this right now and you are not truly helping me.

This is our life I guess for real. So truly, truly thank you for all that you have done for us all including me. I more than appreciate it. Yes I get angry at you but you are the coolest and the greatest of all. I am glad, more than glad and honoured to know you. You are my true friend and protector.

Yes I am walking away as of 2015 January 1, but it does not mean I won't keep in touch with you. Will always keep in touch and be there for you. Thank you for choosing me; but I have to truly step aside and let you and death handle your business.

This isn't the end. It's our new beginning because I still have What a Mess to finish and then some.

Life is worth living, hence I am handing you back good and true life for safe keeping infinitely and indefinitely forever ever without end. And now that California has banned the Confederate Flag, I truly give you back this flag for safe keeping because they truly do not know what they have done. Truly stay true to me and you because I know California will be gone soon. Hence the final separations of lands must be today; now. He must complete the task now that all the flags of life have been given back to you Good God. All the flags of the South have been given back to you accept for those in Africa. I cannot take these flags because they are truly home with you; they belong indefinitely forever ever without end. Know that this is the right decision. So you too must step aside from death and or sins children; sinful and wicked; evil people and spirits and let death do their work accordingly. We cannot stay death anymore because all is compete in my book. Yes the harlot is still there but evil did transfer power to a black man in 2013. He has the scarlet robe; table cloth of death. So the table of death has been set and we cannot change this because this is evil's right and he

Satan and or Evil did exercise his right by transferring his power to a human in the living.

I've been dreaming about different things lately. I can't remember if I dreamt Russia again this week. I had some weird dreams this morning but for some strange reason I can't remember if I dreamt the destruction of another land. Oh well I am so going to leave this alone because I so can't remember.

Going to leave the dream I had about my sister's husband alone as well. If he (my sister's husband) wants to go into the fire with my sister and his children then so be it. I have to live my life and they have to life theirs. Hence I truly need to leave where I am and I know where I want and need to go but I cannot do this; move alone. I need your consent and permission to take this road. I truly need this Good God, hence truly help me because life as we know will not be the same.

Judgment has been passed again by me and in all honesty it is fair; just.

You cannot kill people and expect all to be okay with you. Hence I ask you Good God and Allelujah, how do you look upon man – humanity knowing the sins we have done and do do? How can you say these are my people knowing the sins we commit on a daily basis?

All is life, hence Allelujah – the true Breath of Life. We cannot say we love you and hurt you in this way; so.

We cannot say we love you then turn around and lie to your face. This is not right it's wrong.

We cannot say we have religion and do all in the name of religion that is wrong. We are truly hurting you when we do this. You are our hope and when we kill this hope what do we have left? You are not a religion nor do you lie to anyone. Yes I call you a liar but this is my right with you. Like I said, I made you my all including my beating stick. I would rather make you my all than to make someone else or some other god my all. I know you hence it's you that I come to with my all.

We are nothing without you Good God and we both know this, but yet we as humans choose the folly ground each and every day. Come on now. How can we say we love you and have you, but yet do all to displease and kill you?

How can we say we praise you and thank you, but yet turn around and disobey you? Nothing has changed with you Good God but all has changed for the worse with us humans; man. We sin and disrespect you but yet say you are going to save us all.

How can you save us all when we are not all yours to begin with?

We break every rule and or law and think this is okay when it is not.

You are your people's saving grace Good God and I will not change this.

You are true life and I refuse to give up true life to go to hell and die with death. You are my true right and I exercise my true right by clinging to you stronger than crazy glue and all the glues of this earth and universe including your abode combined. I will not lose you for anyone or anything. So truly keep me stuck to you more than infinitely and indefinitely forever ever without end.

My stepping aside is not an abandonment of you on my part. I just need all this madness to end so that true life can live infinitely and indefinitely in truth, cleanliness, true peace and harmony in a positive and good way forever ever without end indefinitely here on earth and in the spiritual realm.

Sin and death had their time and the time of death is over. So let life; true and good life truly live in goodness and in truth honestly and positively in a good and clean way infinitely and indefinitely forever ever without end. Let us not be subject to anymore sin and evil. We must be good and true to life hence we must live truly clean and help earth in all that we do in a good and true way.

Let the lies of evil be done indefinitely forever ever without end Good God.

So until our next book you take care and we will talk again.

Michelle Jean
October 23, 2014

Dear God can I get old and gray with you?

I mean when I can't go anymore will you be my feet and help me walk?

I am listening to LIVE ON by Beres Hammond and Marcia Griffith and I truly like this song. It does something to me and for me. So can you be my gray headed and old someone sitting with me watching the sunset on a beach somewhere?

Can we truly live on in peace and truth for all eternity?

Can we be truly free so that we can live on and on without end?

Will you break my heart in the end?

Or

Do I have to worry?

Oh Good God how wonderful it is to have you beside me.

Thank you for caring and listening to me.

Michelle Jean
December 07, 2014

My darling, don't take your eyes off me
Let the passion in your eyes undress me
Let the feeling within me flow
Glow

Ah my darling love me tonight and forever
You are my king
My forever ever truth

Touch me
Wrap your love around me
Embrace me with truth
Your true love

Take me to heaven and back
Whisper words of truth, true love in my ears

Take my hand
Keep me forever in your heart
Never lose it
It is divine

Michelle Jean

I need to live on Good God.

I need my unconditional love of truth for you and of you to forever live on and on.

So despite my harsh ways you are truly loved by me.

And to all lovers out there that has that right and true someone, I dedicate PUT IT ON ME by Morgan Heritage to all of you.

Michelle Jean
December 07, 2014

OTHER BOOKS BY MICHELLE JEAN

Blackman Redemption – The Fall of Michelle Jean
Blackman Redemption – After the Fall Apology
Blackman Redemption – World Cry – Christine Lewis
Blackman Redemption
Blackman Redemption – The Rise and Fall of Jamaica
Blackman Redemption – The War of Israel
Blackman Redemption – The Way I Speak to God
Blackman Redemption – A Little Talk With Man
Blackman Redemption – The Den of Thieves
Blackman Redemption – The Death of Jamaica
Blackman Redemption – Happy Mother's Day
Blackman Redemption – The Death of Faith
Blackman Redemption – The War of Religion
Blackman Redemption – The Death of Russia
Blackman Redemption – The Truth
Blackman Redemption – Spiritual War
Blackman Redemption – The Youths
Blackman Redemption – Black Man Where Is Your God?

The New Book of Life
The New Book of Life – A Cry For The Children
The New Book of Life – Judgement
The New Book of Life – Love Bound
The New Book of Life – Me
The New Book of Life – Life

Just One of Those Days
Book Two – Just One of Those Days
Just One of Those Days – Book Three The Way I Feel
Just One of Those Days – Book Four

The Days I Am Weak
Crazy Thoughts – My Book of Sin
Broken
Ode to Mr. Dean Fraser

A Little Little Talk
A Little Little Talk – Book Two

Prayers
My Collective
A Little Talk/A Time For Fun and Play
Simple Poems
Behind The Scars
Songs of Praise And Love

Love Bound
Love Bound – Book Two

Dedication Unto My Kids
More Talk
Saving America From A Woman's Perspective
My Collective the Other Side of Me

My Collective the Dark Side of Me
A Blessed Day
Lose To Win
My Doubtful Days – Book One

My Little Talk With God
My Little Talk With God – Book Two

A Different Mood and World – Thinking

My Nagging Day
My Nagging Day – Book Two

Friday September 13, 2013
My True Love
It Would Be You
My Day

A Little Advice – Talk
1313, 2032, 2132 – The End of Man
Tata

MICHELLE'S BOOK BLOG – BOOKS 1 – 19

My Problem Day
A Better Way
Stay – Adultery and the Weight of Sin – Cleanliness Message

Let's Talk
Lonely Days – Foundation
A Little Talk With Jamaica – As Long As I Live
Instructions For Death
My Lonely Thoughts